In Praise of

Marathon Fit to Lead

"Mike Matte is a fantastic speaker who inspired and energized my employees to grow our company and take it to the next level. He helped us to understand that by becoming "marathon fit," we improve our own lives as well as the performance of our company. In this book, Mike shares lessons that will help you to run your best life."

Phil Morabito, President & CEO
Pierpont Communications

"Great leaders are defined by the way they respond to the difficult challenges that occur on their watch. Mike Matte understands that the events are only 10 percent, and it's the way you respond that really matters. I recommend this book to people who are looking to make positive changes at home, at work and in their communities."

Clay Ford
Representative, District 3
Florida House of Representatives
Colonel, US Army (Retired)

"There is something special about Marathon Fit to Lead. What sets Mike Matte apart is his authenticity as he shares his intensely personal story as a marathon runner and company CEO. This book offers a genuinely refreshing perspective and uncommon insight into life's challenges and the way we respond."

Bob Greifeld
Chairman, USA Track & Field Foundation
CEO, NASDAQ OMX
New York, NY

"Mike Matte will inspire you to live your best life possible as he takes you along on his marathon. With humility, humor and a passion for helping others, he shares his own life stories of struggle, persistence and victory so that you, too, can set meaningful goals and live with a sense of purpose"

Ruben Gonzalez
Four-time Olympian, Business Author, Speaker

Marathon Fit to Lead

26.2 Transformational Leadership
Ideas to Help You Run Your Best Life....NOW!

Mike Matte
The Marathon CEO

**Foreword by
Admiral Tom Lynch**

Marathon
Fit to Lead

26.2 Transformational Leadership Ideas to Help You Run Your Best Life...NOW!

Mike Matte
The Marathon CEO

Foreword by
Admiral Tom Lynch

Marathon Fit to Lead
26.2 Transformational Leadership
Ideas to Help You Run Your Best Life....NOW!

Mike Matte, The Marathon CEO www.MarathonCEO.com
Houston, TX

By Mike Matte, The Marathon CEO
All Rights Reserved © 2010 by Mike Matte

Published by Willard St. Publishers
Printed in the United States of America
www.marathonceo.com

Author: Mike Matte
Book and Cover Design: Mike Svat

13-digit ISBN: 9780984310692
10-digit ISBN: 0-9843106-9-X

Library of Congress Control Number: 2010935646

1. Business, Economics 2. Health, Fitness, Beauty
3. Sports
First Edition: September 2010

This book is available at special quantity discounts to use as premiums and sales promotions, or for use in corporate trainings or as conference materials.

For more information, please contact Mike Matte at
www.MarathonCEO.com
Or contact Director of Special Sales at Willard Street Publishing
1302 Waugh Dr. #344 Houston, TX 77019

To
Jennifer,
Megan,
Melissa,
Jason
and Cole

Acknowledgements

There are many people who have worked to make this book a success and I want to extend to them my thanks and recognition for their contributions. This project has been a true marathon, and it has required stamina, sustained focus and patience.

No one can run a marathon without the support of family and friends and I want to thank my parents, Bob and Martha Matte, for instilling the values and discipline that got me started and kept me running.

While much of "Marathon Fit to Lead...," is about my marathon, I also want to extend my thanks to Jane Luco, Sherri Cothrun and Larry Lichnovsky for generously sharing their marathon stories as well.

This book would not have happened without Sue Howard, Pattie McKenna and Mike Svat. They each brought their unique talents to this marathon – putting the stories into the written word, creating the images of my marathon; their help in the publishing process has been integral.

There are others who have helped me on this marathon that deserve special mention: Ruben Gonzalez, Tom Jackovic, Phil Morabito, Leslie S. Randall, and Jan Wilson have all helped to bring this project to conclusion.

But most of all I want to recognize my wife Sharon who has been with me every step of my marathon to launch my career as an international speaker and author. None of this could have happened without her. Thank you, honey.

Foreword

It's a fundamental fact that life will present some difficult moments. These are the times that Mike Matte calls the 10 percent events. It's the 90 percent, the way you respond, that makes the difference. It's the 90 percent response, the way you go forward, that people will remember.

Throughout his life, Mike Matte has kept going forward. As a skinny-kid-turned-athlete, as a military officer commanding a squadron on high alert, as a corporate CEO turning around failing operations and – finally – as a marathon runner – Mike Matte has kept his life on track.

In *Marathon Fit To Lead. 26.2 Transformational Leadership Ideas To Help You Run Your Best Life… NOW!*, Mike generously shares his marathon in hopes it will inspire you to get going, to keep going forward, and to give your best 90 percent response to all the events in your own life. His stories are sad, funny, inspirational and touching, They should be required reading for anyone who wants to live the best life possible and who would like a companion for support along the way. When you read this book, you'll feel Mike's pain – you'll also feel his humor and joy.

Mike will help you see things in your life that may have slipped to the side. He'll help you identify your dreams. He'll help you discover your strengths. And then he'll be by your side as you use those strengths to set goals and make your dreams come true. He does this by offering more than his personal views; he offers his own real life story. He tells you how he got started as a high school athlete with a father for a coach, how he got dates as a military cadet when the military was at its lowest popularity, and how he kept going as a young manager when all he wanted to do was to quit.

Thousands of individuals have heard Mike as a public speaker and have been inspired and strengthened by his message and unflagging spirit. He gets people out of their seats, cheering YES! He is eloquent in both the spoken and the written word.

In *Marathon Fit To Lead. 26.2 Transformational Leadership Ideas To Help You Run Your Best Life... NOW!*, Mike will help you to see that you, too, are on a marathon and that if you embrace that concept, your life will be better for it. Whether you're starting a business, struggling with the tough economy or training for the 26.2-mile race, he'll speak to you.

Listen to him. He'll help you get there.

Admiral Tom Lynch

Mile Markers

Introduction

Life is a Marathon

"An object at rest tends to stay at rest, and an object in motion tends to stay in motion."

Sir Isaac Newton's First Law of Motion

Regardless of whether or not you're a runner, as I am, you're always in a marathon. Life is a marathon, and it requires the same level of preparation, training, commitment, and perseverance as running the 26.2 mile race. The concepts you are about to learn in this book are what I call the 'marathon strategy.' They've been applied to long-distance running, but are just as applicable to running a business, an organization, and your life. This marathon strategy has helped many people become more successful, more fulfilled, and better able to overcome life's little, and big, surprises that inevitably emerge along the way. Some surprises can literally stop you in your tracks.

You didn't expect your IRA to evaporate. You didn't expect that you would have to work beyond the age of 65. You didn't expect the value of your home to be less than what you're paying for it. And speaking of your houses, you sure didn't expect, at this stage, to be living with your kids...They're back!

Think about the surprises that have come the way of the 10 million Americans who have watched their jobs disappear, and with them, their salaries, group health insurance, and employer contributions to their retirement fund. Think about the millions of people who have lost their homes to foreclosure.

My point simply is that marathons can be mind-numbing. They can be painful, daunting, and extremely discouraging. Sometimes, you can become so overwhelmed you forget you are on a marathon and that someday it will be over. You check out, drift into autopilot, and instead of running your marathon, your marathon runs you. You are no longer mentally focused, emotionally connected, physically energized, or spiritually aligned with your purpose. As you get dragged along, you forget that your time is finite, that there is a day when you will no longer be here. You forget there will come a time when you will no longer be on the marathon that is uniquely yours to run. You don't need to search far and wide to see that a staggering number of Americans have stopped running their marathons. Statistics show that most people are mentally engaged with their work only half the time they are on the job. We don't understand our emotions and swing from happy to mad, to glad to sad, and back around again without knowing why. We lack a spiritual sense of purpose, and we don't take care of ourselves. Experts estimate that only one in 10 American adults exercise regularly.

Perhaps most disturbing is the effect on our children. According to the Centers for Disease Control, obesity has tripled among 6 to 19-year-olds and doubled among 2 to 5-year-olds in the past three decades. The National Institute of Health has published a report forecasting the first sustained drop in life expectancy in modern history because of the rapid rise in obesity. That means that for the first time, children will, on the average, live shorter lives than their parents. That's not a legacy I want to leave to the next generations.

Where do you see yourself in this scenario? Are you participating in your marathon? Or rather than being fully involved in your life and work, have you become passive, standing on the sidelines and watching as each day passes you by? Have you lost your inspiration and motivation to get up each day and be fully engaged in life? Maybe you got surprised and never recuperated from the setback. Or maybe you became disillusioned after running aimlessly for years without the right tools and training to make your life's marathon profitable and rewarding. If so, I want to help you to get moving again, to become a participant in your life, instead of an observer of it.

Throughout my career, as well as my life, I've used principles that are known to many. One of those principles was introduced by a stuffy, but intelligent, man who discovered the laws of motion. Sir Isaac Newton's First Law of Motion states that an object at rest tends to stay at rest, and an object in motion tends to stay in motion.

Newton's First Law of Motion is a fitting description of my life. I've been in motion for decades. Like you, I've had setbacks and experienced a few stalls along my journey, but I've never let it stop my momentum for long. You might know me as the Marathon CEO and a speaker who travels from coast to coast to share the universal principles I've learned with others in hopes of inspiring them to start running their own marathons.

With every mile of the journey and every stop along the way, there is always an opportunity to learn. Around every bend is a new experience, a new person, and new possibilities. But to find them, you have to get moving. You have to prepare yourself for the active pursuit of your dreams and goals. This book is intended to inspire you to run your marathon by re-engaging mentally, emotionally, physically, and spiritually—by living your life fully, setting goals, and making conscious decisions.

The unexpected events in your life are not what you are all about. They do not define you. They are simply milestones, or mile markers, on your journey. What counts, what people will remember, is how you respond. The event is only 10 percent of the experience; the way you respond is the 90 percent.

Heading out the door for a long run has always been my response to the unexpected. On September 11, 2001, when people everywhere were glued to their TVs watching the devastation of the World Trade Center, I processed my grief and horror by pounding the pavement. Speeding along the deserted streets of downtown Forth Worth, the world was eerily silent; the only sound was the soft slap of my feet on the dry pavement. It was like I was the only soul on earth. But in front of every high-rise building stood cadres of security guards, who turned toward me with stony, blank stares as I ran by. The world was suddenly expecting the unexpected that day, and a lone, skinny guy running their way was cause for concern, even suspicion.

I've kept running through pain, injuries, setbacks, disappointments, and the unexpected, because I choose to keep my marathon alive. I hope you do, too. In this book, you'll learn the same principles I follow in my marathon. I invite you to accompany me on my journey back to my youth in rural northern Illinois, to my military days when I was confronted by the confusion and controversy of Viet Nam, and more recently, to my experiences as an executive charged with turning around failing operations only to become the new guy in the outplacement office. I hope you'll be inspired and gain your own momentum through the stories of people I admire; they've set and achieved amazing goals; they've kept moving forward, despite the unexpected.

The principles of marathon running that I share with you combine to form the starting point from which you can approach everything in life. They have served me well on all the legs of my journey. In this book, I turn them over to you with the hope that they will support and inspire you to live consciously and run your marathon as only you can. An object in motion tends to stay in motion, but in order for that to happen, you have to take the first step.

Run your marathon—run your life,

Mike Matte

mile
one

The First Step

"Faith is taking the first step,
even when you don't see the whole staircase."

Martin Luther King, Jr.

The path you've taken in your life leaves traces – footsteps that reveal where you've been and the stops you've made along the way. They show when you've paused, feet still and firmly planted side by side, as well as the times you've changed direction. But regardless what traces you've left behind, there is one undeniable truth – in order to leave tracks you had to get moving. You had to take the first step.

The first step is monumental. It's as important and celebratory as a baby's first step. Without it, nothing happens. Whether you're interested in training for your first marathon or you know it's time to make a big change in your life or career, you won't accomplish anything until you take the first step.

My running career started on a cinder track that I built with my Dad and my brother Billy. We'd go down to the boiler room at Marengo High School where Dad coached track and we'd shovel the coal ash out of the furnace. We'd transport it in a wheelbarrow to the field where we carved a track out of the grass. We'd unload the oily black pile, rake it over the dirt and flatten it with a big, heavy roller. Then we'd go back for more.

I was a freshman and my Dad was my coach. I was small for an athlete – 5 foot, 10 inches, 140 pounds – and not particularly fast. But I could keep going... and going... and going. I ran on that black, grimy surface every day through every kind of weather northern Illinois had to offer – golden crisp autumn sunshine, soft grey silent snow showers, icy bone-numbing sleet and drenching spring rain.

My running career got established in my freshman year of high school with my Dad as my coach, but my marathon started the day I entered the dank, musty darkness of the Marengo High School boiler room with a wheelbarrow and a shovel, determined to build a running track. That's when I took my first step.

The first step on your marathon is the hardest... and most important. Whether you're training for your first 26.2-mile race or making a big change in your life or career, you won't accomplish anything until you take the first step. There is distance between you and your goal, and obstacles to overcome. After all, before I could even embark on my goal to run competitively, I needed a track. It's up to you to close the gap by taking action, even if you have to pick up a shovel and haul cinder.

Your first step will set everything in motion. Like a gear, it will propel the next step, the next and the next. Don't get caught up in the details – if we had thought about the number of wheelbarrow trips it would take to complete the track in Marengo we might not have gotten started. Instead, we freed our minds and we moved forward trusting that we were taking the first step, just one of many, that would put Marengo on the track and field circuit. The first step, just one of many, that would get me to the finish line of a 26.2-mile race.

Since then, running has been the catapult to change in my life. When I put on my shoes, my mind set changes. Rather than fretting about something that happened that day, I go for a run. When my legs move, I process information constructively and put things in perspective. I know that if I don't run, I'll begin to worry. Thoughts will spin round and round in my head and I'll get stuck.

That's what happened early in my corporate career. I was working all the time, using all my energy to turn around a failing company and I was a new father of a colicky baby girl. I let circumstances take control; I let problems take time away from my daily running regimen and as time passed, I stopped running entirely. It didn't take long for paralysis to set in. I was in a rut and I became overcome with anxiety.

To this day I thank the Human Resources Vice President at corporate headquarters who gave me the tools to get started again. Instead of a shovel and a pile of coal, he offered a team building course and a set of inspirational tapes by Dr. Denis Waitley, entitled "The Psychology of Winning." I got back in touch with the mind/body relationship and how exercise reduces stress and anxiety. I remembered how it felt when endorphins are released in my body.

Denis Waitley's words inspired me to set goals and get moving again. I started running and within 60 days I dropped 10 pounds, not to mention the stress. My energy level increased and I became better able to focus on solutions, rather than getting overwhelmed by problems. I became a better husband and father and a better leader at work. The employees responded well to the new me and became more engaged. Within 24 months, we turned the failing company around.

You may have been feeling the need to change yourself, perhaps for a long time. Yet you haven't taken the first step. You may be stuck in a rut and intimidated by what you see as your first hurdle. It's too difficult to leave behind the routine, the familiar. There's too much to do; you don't have the time or the concentration you need to break old habits.

But if you don't start moving, each day that passes

without action will make the goal seem more distant. It may begin to seem even impossible. I promise you that reaching your goal, whatever it is, is not impossible.

If you push aside the inertia and get moving, you will have taken the first step. Whether you want to be a long-distance runner, a mountain climber, an author or salesperson of the year, you can't get going until you take the first step. It's the hardest point of the journey but it's the one that produces the most reward because you'll be moving.

It's your marathon, your life, pursue it.

Get started! Go!

Exercise:

List your goals, and below each one, identify one thing you can do today toward achieving them. Then as the saying goes, do it!

1.   Goal: ....

....

      Step One: ....

2.   Goal: ....

....

      Step One: ....

3.   Goal: ....

....

      Step One: ....

mile
two

Visualize Your Success

"When you rehearse success in your mind, you experience it in your life."

Remez Sasson

Now that you're moving, you're on your way! What was once unlikely is now possible because you've taken action. The doors that now open offer exciting new opportunities, limited by only one thing—the scope of your thoughts. So, after you take that first step, unleash your mind. Whether you're running or pursuing another goal, let your mind run free, as well. A goal is a major stepping stone in life, and much like a marathon, you have to believe that you can and you will complete it.

Napoleon Hill, possibly the greatest success philosopher in history, said, "What the mind of man can conceive and believe, it can achieve." Everything starts with a thought. Before you could take that first step, your mind was in motion, creating a dream. You turned that dream into a goal, but unless your mind conceived it, you wouldn't have been inspired to do anything at all. This is true not only in influencing the first step in pursuit of our dream and goals, but also in the level of success we'll achieve down the road.

If your mind can envision success, it can achieve it. If your mind can envision great triumphs, you can accomplish it. First, though, allow your imagination to conjure up your own unique vision of success. Think of your mind as a huge canvas on which you can paint your own vivid portrait of success. Including the finest details, create a picture of you reaching your goal. What will you look like? Where will you be? What will you be doing? What will you see, smell, and taste? Will you be celebrating, or do you see yourself as peaceful and introspective? What sounds will you hear? Imagine yourself crossing the finish line...

The sting of the tape giving way across your chest...

The shock of ice water thrown from the coolers...

The sound of the race official calling your name and number over the microphone...

The cheers...

The weight of the medal resting against your chest...

The tears in your father's eyes as he grins with pride on the sideline.

Creating that vision of success in your mind makes it real. Because you can experience it, you tend to want it more. Without that vision, it's too vague and, therefore, you won't have the driving motivation to make it happen. After all, you don't crave a certain food if you're never tasted it, right? You wouldn't have an intense desire to have a certain car if you'd never seen or driven the car, would you? The same is true for goals; once you envision and experience them, you naturally want them more and will do what it takes to bring them to reality. You'll want to do what it takes to feel the sting of the tape, to hear your name, and to see the swell of pride in your family's faces.

Training for a marathon takes discipline and dedication. I've found that keeping a crisp, clear picture of the outcome in front of me at all times motivates me to keep running toward it. The same philosophy applies to life, whether it's family, career, or success goals. What element of your life, career, or success can you visualize and then focus on achieving? Figure out what it is that you want and then create a vision in all its grandeur of how it will feel. That vision gives you something concrete to work toward, and when you add emotional attachment to it, you'll move mountains to get there. As author and speaker Brian Tracy says, "you have to see your bull's eye before you can hit it."

See it. Feel it. Believe it.

Exercise:

Set your goal, then let your mind paint a vivid picture of the moment when you achieve it. Write down precisely how it will feel, where you will be, who will be with you, the sounds, sights, tastes, and emotions that accompany it. Be vivid and colorful in your descriptions.

Goal: ....

....

....

I feel ....

....

I see ....

....

I hear ....

....

I taste ....

....

I touch ....

....

mile
three

Put Yourself First

"Remember, you are your own best friend, so you'd better take care of yourself first."

Super Girl

Like putting your best foot forward, real success in life requires putting yourself first. That doesn't mean that you have to be selfish or inconsiderate of others. On the contrary, it means that you can't take care of anyone or anything unless you take care of yourself. In order to give your best to other people and to your own endeavors, you need to be physically, mentally, and emotionally able to do so.

Marathons drain you mentally, emotionally, physically and spiritually, and so do life's responsibilities and demands. Providing for your family, making a positive impact on the job in the midst of spending cutbacks, caring for an ailing parent, or launching a job search in a bad economy requires commitment and sustainable energy. Top that with all of the daily chores and other demands on your time, and it's understandable that sometimes there simply isn't enough of you to go around. When you're drained and zapped, something has to give.

The more your marathon demands of you, the more you need to put yourself at the top of your list every day. You simply can't be there for others if you haven't taken care of yourself. The longer you attempt to do so, the more you and those around you will suffer. If you physically exert yourself without eating right and getting sufficient rest, you won't have the strength or stamina to sustain your performance. Eventually, your body will send out warning signals telling you that you're overtired, undernourished, or overstrained. And the effects aren't only physical; you'll be drained emotionally and mentally and your relationships with family, co-workers and friends may also suffer as well. If you're burning both ends of the candle and squeezing in a few extra hours into an already packed day, you may also invite extra stress into your life. It's well known that stress causes nervousness, headaches, stomach problems, and high blood pressure, to name a few problems. You need to take something off your plate. Learn to say no, learn how to delegate. There's nothing wrong with asking for help. Learn how to relax. Give yourself a break, literally, and breathe deeply, clearing your mind of the constant reminders of the things you have to do. It will do wonders for your outlook, attitude, and your effectiveness.

Putting yourself first will help you to keep moving forward. It will keep you in top-notch shape so you can meet the demands of your marathon. Yes, you are worth it. In fact, you owe it to yourself and to the people who depend on you to give them the best that you've got. You can't do that if you fail to take care of you.

There was a point in my life when I stopped taking care of myself. I was overwhelmed with mounting responsibilities at work. Being the youngest employee in charge of a struggling company demanded long hours at work and very little time off. At home, my wife had given birth to our first child. I told myself that I had no time for me and I stopped running. Everything went downhill from there. I was frustrated and burdened with so much stress that I finally gave up. "I can't do this anymore," I told the Human Resources Vice President at company headquarters. "I'm turning in my resignation."

Rather than accepting it, he sent me to a self-help seminar that reminded me of the importance of taking care of myself. Only then, would I be able to take care of my job, the employees who depended on me, and my family who needed me. I laced up my shoes and started running again. It was the best decision in my life. Getting exercise and taking time to do something I loved helped me put other things into perspective. As I set an even and steady pace, the pace of my life seemed to even out as well. I could see things more clearly and find solutions, instead of being so overwhelmed by problems that I couldn't deal with anything. In short, life became manageable again when I finally began to manage my life according to my needs.

Returning to running made me physically healthier and stronger, and it reduced the emotional stress and mental duress I'd placed on myself. The effects were almost immediate, and the company I'd been hired to turn around responded positively. I learned to delegate and I saw great results. I learned that in order to give my best to others, I had to give myself the same consideration.

Be good to yourself. Respect your body and mind and understand the consequences of what you are asking yourself to do. Learn the importance of saying no if you truly have too much on your plate, or ask for help. Schedule alone-time to relax and recuperate from stress. Get some rest and create a balance in your work, family, and social life. Do something that makes you laugh. Put you first, and you'll be amazed by all you can do for others.

Exercise:

Make a log of your day. How much time are you spending on your responsibilities? List how many hours were spent on work, on home and family obligations, on community and social requests. When you're done, review your log. Did you eat on the run? Did you take a 15- or 20-minute break and use it to relax? Did you have any time or energy left to do one thing you truly enjoyed today? Did you remember to exercise and get a good night's sleep? If you weren't able to do those things, are there tasks on that list that someone else can do or tasks that weren't totally necessary?

After opening a window in your day, determine how you would like to use that time. Would you go for a walk? How about a run? Would you visit friends, golf, read a book, play with your children, or take up an old hobby? Why not do it? When you find time to do things you enjoy, the rest of your life becomes more enjoyable, too.

Notes:

_____

_____

_____

_____

_____

_____

mile
four

Plan Your Route

"Standing in the
middle of the road is very dangerous;
you get knocked down by
the traffic from both sides."

Margaret Thatcher

When you set out on a long journey, you don't leave things to chance. You get a map. You plan a route. You decide how far you want to get each day. You make reservations to stay overnight. You calculate the time it will take to get there and how long you're going to stay.

A plan will get you to your destination.

You wouldn't hop into a car for a weekend trip without having an idea which direction you're going, would you? If you do, you're not going to arrive at your destination for a long time. You'll be traveling in circles, backtracking the path you've already followed, or even worse, left stuck in the middle of the road without a clue which way to go.

Make a plan. Plan a route. Have an ultimate destination. Only then will you be able to gauge your progress and determine if you're on the right path. Your plan is there to keep you moving forward and to tell you the next step to take. It's the tool you'll use to measure your past progress and to calculate your future. Without it, you won't have any idea if you're nearing your destination or moving farther from it.

The first time you set out on a run, you're likely to have

a plan. You know if you're going to run around the block or around the gym. You have an idea how far you're going to run, as well. Are you going to run half a mile, then turn around, or are you going to run two miles and walk back? The plan you make gives you milestones to reach that signify you've met your goal and run your distance.

Everyone needs the almighty plan. In college, you're required to have a plan called a major in order to determine the route you'll take to get to your ultimate goal—a degree in a particular field. In life, you need a plan as well, to make sure you arrive on time to meetings or have sufficient funds for your children's education or retirement. We welcome plans in every phase of our life - pension plans, business plans, agendas, blueprints, and career plans. Why leave the rest of your marathon to chance?

Whether you're training for your first marathon or revamping your company, make a plan and map your progress. When you're planning your route, decide which direction you want to go and what roads you'll take, always keeping in mind your ultimate destination. Then, determine what the terrain will be like—is it uphill or flat, is it likely that you'll encounter more bumps in the road if you choose a particular route? Will one route take longer than another? Are there points of interest along the way that will provide extra benefits? You might want to choose the path of least resistance. Whether it is a rest stop or a partner who will join you on your path, there are amenities that will make your journey easier and more enjoyable. Or you may prefer a path that will build your stamina, strength and endurance, knowing that it will condition you for greater challenges down the road. Consider all of these, along with the obstacles, challenges, or hurdles you may have to jump on a particular route.

Above all, a plan helps you control your progress. Rather than spinning your wheels, you know precisely where you want to be and how you're going to get there. That puts you far ahead of the average person, who goes through life without a goal or a destination.

Once you plan your route, you'll have something which will help you measure your progress. Review it often to determine if your plan is moving you forward at the pace you'd like or if there are challenges that may require you to take another path. Do you need to increase your speed to meet your goal or have you found that some of the steps you've mapped aren't necessary? The beauty of the plan is that it's yours, and you have the control over it. It's never written in stone, however, it is a firm guide that will point you in the right direction and propel you forward, rather than taking one step forward and two steps back.

Keep moving forward with a plan that keeps you on track to reach your goals. Knowing where you're going is one thing—knowing precisely how you're going to get there will make the trip faster, easier, and far more enjoyable. Take control of your marathon. Plan your route.

If you've been stuck, it's time to get out of the middle of the road and start moving in one direction or another. Make a plan, plan your route, and the ride will go much more smoothly.

Exercise:

Set two goals, one for running or another feat you'd like to accomplish, and another for your life. Where do you want to be next year, in five, ten, or twenty years? Then break it down, determine how far you will go in increments of time, setting particular goals along your journey that you can use to measure your progress.

mile
five

Prepare

"I have yet to be in a game where luck was involved.
Well-prepared players make plays.
I have yet to be in a game where the most prepared
team didn't win."

Urban Meyer

You wouldn't run a marathon without a good pair of running shoes, would you? Of course not. You're going to make sure you're properly equipped with the things you need, like running clothes, socks, shoes, drinks, etc. Before you step out the door, you'd ensure that you're prepared for the run you are about to take. You want to feel confident that you have had sufficient training and preparation for the distance you want to cover.

Running a marathon isn't something you can just jump into. Seasoned runners know how much training and preparation goes into such a major feat, and they know that marathons require extensive mental and physical preparation. The same is also true for success in any pursuit. Success doesn't happen by accident. It's not about luck, either. You don't just appear at the right place at the right time and find yourself at the top of the corporate ladder. You also don't wake up one morning and, lo and behold, you've shed 20 pounds since you went to bed. Those are things that come as the result of commitment, preparation, and more than a little bit of work.

People who enter a marathon get there because they've

devoted months or even years to preparing for it. People who are successful get there because they prepare for success. There is little difference. By preparing themselves, they are conditioning their mind and body with the experience, education, and motivation that will bring their goal to fruition.

How does one prepare for success? They get the proper education and learn the skills they'll need. They seek the advice and guidance of others who are already successful to give them a leg up on the competition. They master the art of visualizing success to the point where they can taste and feel it. Successful people keep their goal within sight at all times, and they know if they lose focus of it, they'll encounter setbacks.

Preparation for success starts very young in life. As a child, you prepared to enter school by learning the alphabet and getting supplies. You prepared for tests by listening in class, taking notes, and studying. You prepared for sports events by getting the proper equipment, going to practices and listening to your coach. You prepare for a job interview by preparing a resume and learning about the company, dressing appropriately and marketing your skills and experience. Everything you do requires preparation, including making a meal. So, it's not surprising that success would require some level of preparation, too.

The level of success you will achieve is in direct correlation to the amount of preparation you make. The more you prepare, the better prepared you will be when opportunity knocks. Whether you're running your marathon or your life, the greatest rewards and achievements will come as the direct result of the preparation you give to it. Preparing to succeed requires a positive attitude, commitment, and focus on your goal. If you were to invite negativity and doubt into your preparation, you're not preparing to succeed, but preparing to fail.

Preparation not only gets you to your destination, but once you're there, it keeps you there. It's rare that anyone becomes an overnight success. Like playing the lottery, it's a gamble you can't count on. Those who do become wealthy through the lottery sometimes find themselves destitute later in life. That's because they didn't gain the knowledge and experience that preparation provides, so once they had wealth, they didn't know how to keep it.

There are stories of many entrepreneurs who amassed fortunes, only to lose them at some point. Donald Trump was one such millionaire who filed bankruptcy, but he was able to rebuild his empire because the years of preparation he'd put into his success gave him the knowledge and experience to repeat his success.

I prepare for every run, trip, and project I undertake. The training I received when I entered the Air Force in 1971 prepared me for Viet Nam and resulted in an eight-year military career. That experience prepared me as I entered the business world and gave me the tools I needed to pick myself up when I suddenly lost my job and livelihood. All of my experiences prepared me for speaking and my career as the Marathon CEO. During all of it, running has been a mainstay in my preparation. Running has continually helped me make major decisions and find solutions. It has given me the mind-set and the tools to push myself through tough times and to dig deeper to reach my goals.

Don't let your life be the victim of chance. Prepare for it. Decide where you want to go, make a plan, mark your route and then give yourself the training you'll need to get there. The proper preparation will move you forward, mile by mile, on your marathon.

Exercise

Go back and revisit the goals you wrote in the Mile Four exercise. List the preparation you'll need in the following areas:

1. Education/Knowledge:

2. Tools/Supplies:

3. Amount of Training and Experience:

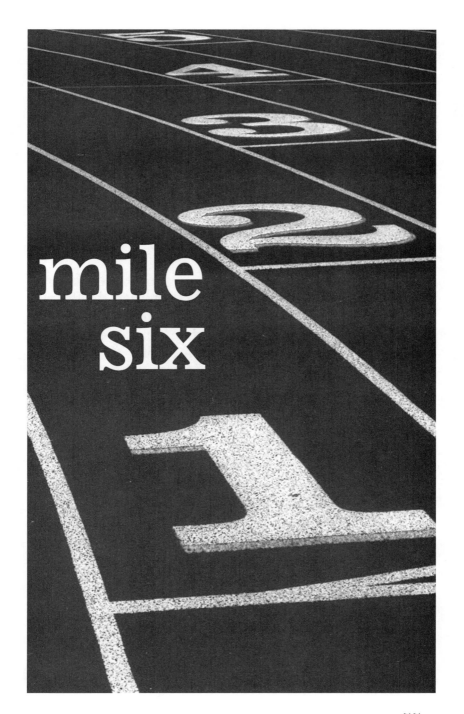

mile
six

The First Marathon

"We gain strength, and courage, and confidence by each experience in which we really stop to look fear in the face...we must do that which we think we cannot."

Eleanor Roosevelt

You've done everything right. You've created a vision of your success, set the goals that will get you there, built a plan and got yourself prepared. Important achievements require that you train, and running a marathon is no exception. Now it's time to use all that you've done. Are you ready to take the leap? It's time to step out with faith in yourself, knowing you're prepared, knowing you can accomplish your goal and overcome any obstacles that get in your way.

You get that faith from knowing that you've done all you can to be ready. It may be tough, even when you've trained for years, but the tough challenges are the most rewarding. It's also when you build the best memories.

Trust that you're ready for your marathon and allow yourself to get that feeling of anticipation that pumps you up at the starting line. Yes, this is something new. You haven't done it before, and you're excited to get started. Today is your big day, and all of the preparation you've done up to this point made it happen. All of the time, sweat, aches, and pains that conditioned you for the big race don't matter anymore. You're ready.

Enjoy the anticipation for this "first" in your life when you begin, and use your excitement to keep you energized and determined when you begin to tire. At some point, you may feel disillusioned. The wind won't always be at your back, and your journey won't be all downhill. So, let your emotional investment push you through the physical or mental challenges you'll face along the way. Your emotions can provide the fuel you need to keep going forward, especially under tough conditions. Your emotions provide the adrenalin that will take you to the finish line.

I cherish the memory of my first marathon. I'd been training for a long time. I had competed in lots of races already as a high school student, a cadet in the Air Force and in the military. I had competed at the state level in track and field. I knew that it was time for me to take on the challenge of running in a marathon. My training had given me strength, speed and stamina, and I was running 6-minute miles. So I set my sites on Chicago.

Chicago is a beautiful city by anyone's definition; it was a spectacular place for me to run my first marathon. As I waited impatiently, surrounded by other marathoners as excited as I was, I looked out on Lake Michigan and conjured up my vision of making it to the finish.

I had listened prior to the race to seasoned marathon runners who advised that my training regimen include only 20 miles at my 6.15-per-mile speed. Pushing harder than that would cause too much wear and tear, they said. Instead, they advised, "Save your strength for the last 6.2 miles on the day of the marathon."

Now it was time for the real thing, I thought – 26.2 miles.

The starting gun roared, and we were off.

From the starting line at Grant Park, north to Addison and back downtown – I was making my time. I had three things to look forward to: finishing successfully, making my time, and seeing my dad at the finish line. That's where he was waiting.... Did I tell you he had a stopwatch?

As I passed the 20-mile mark on Halsted, I was going strong. I chugged through Chinatown, still on time. I was a couple of miles short of the finish line, with the massive, brilliant blue sparkle of Lake Michigan to my right.

That's when I made a stunning discovery.

"I can't feel my legs," I thought.

My brain started transmitting bizarre information.

"Don't look down," it said. "Your legs are gone. You have nothing to run on. Don't look down. They're not there."

Then I saw the image of my dad; the legendary coach who'd built championship teams throughout Illinois, the father who would accept nothing but my best in track, basketball, and football. Dad, at the finish line with his stopwatch. The last two miles were the hardest I had ever run, but giving up was not an option. With no feelings in my legs, I ran the last two miles at 7.25 minutes each. As I crossed the finish line, I saw Dad click his stopwatch and wave it in the air. There was a huge grin on his face, and I saw the tears in his eyes.

It was the image of my dad at the finish line that pushed me through the roughest part of the race, the image of my dad that carried me over the finish line. He didn't know that, but I did.

Your marathon is waiting, too. It won't be easy—it never is. But it will be worth every second of training, preparation, and effort that you put into it. And the rewards will be as sweet as you can imagine.

You're ready to run your first marathon, and cross the finish line. Now proudly step out with faith in yourself and do it.

Make a memory!

mile
seven

Not All Marathons
Are Alike

"Our greatest strength as a human race is our ability
to acknowledge our differences;
our greatest weakness is our failure to embrace
them."

Judith Henderson

No two marathons are alike, the same as no two jobs, relationships, or people are alike. From one marathon to another,
you'll encounter different people, environments, atmospheres,
and protocols. Being aware of the similarities and differences
can be critical to your success.

You need to be prepared for this particular marathon—
not the last one. If you switch employers within the same field,
your job probably will not be identical to the last one. You'll
need to learn new things and find out what sets one company
apart from another. Each leg of your marathon and your life
will require you to be prepared for something new, unexpected,
or unique. When you know what's on the horizon, you can better prepare for it.

After you've made it through your first marathon, you
might think you're now a seasoned runner who can easily adapt
to your next marathon. But, each race is different, held at different times of the year and in different areas of the country.
Your second marathon might be worlds apart from your first
one, and the best thing you can do is know what to expect so

you can adapt your training, preparation, and pace accordingly.

Running in the Boston Marathon had long been a dream, and I was excited to have the opportunity to bring it to fruition. The Chicago Marathon qualified me for Boston, and I excitedly started training in November. I ran through anything the brutal Midwestern winter threw my way: blizzard conditions, sleet, freezing rain, and single-digit temperatures. Anyone who has spent a winter in the Midwest knows the extremes of Old Man Winter, and I believed that if I could endure those conditions, I'd be prepared for just about anything.

When I arrived in Boston, it was 45 degrees. But on Patriot's Day, the day of the race, Boston awoke to unseasonably warm spring temperatures. By the time the marathon started, the sun was blazing and the mercury on the thermometer read 72 degrees.

Up until that day, my marathon had been virtually problem-free. I hadn't suffered through injuries or fatigue. I had qualified for Boston having run just one previous marathon. So, while I had trained, I admittedly wasn't an experienced, seasoned marathon runner. Up to this point, for the most part, my marathon had been uneventful and smooth sailing, but I hadn't taken into account that there would be differences between my first marathon and my second. This oversight was not a small one.

The Chicago Marathon course had been flat; Boston was hilly. Chicago started at seven in the morning, just as the sun was rising; Boston started at noon when the sun was high in the sky. The weather in Chicago had been cool, an ideal 49 degrees; Boston in comparison was hot.

Ten miles into the race, the heat got to me and I threw up. When you're pushing your body for 26.2 miles, you need coolant; your body can't do it all by itself. You need a chill in the air and fluids. You can build up your tolerance for a marathon in the fall since you will have trained through the warm summer months, but I was used to the cold. It was readily apparent that I wasn't prepared for 72 degrees. I was dizzy, discouraged and sick, and I was forced to slow down.

I crossed the finish line in Boston with a disappointing time of three hours and 17 minutes. My Dad put his arm around my shoulder and guided me to a nearby maple tree, and disillusioned and disappointed, I sprawled on the grass, my back propped up against the rough bark of the trunk.

On the flight home, I passed out, surrounded by other marathon runners who were in better shape than I was. They'd gone to the medical tent after the race to get intravenous fluids to replenish their body. Since I had never been sick before, it hadn't occurred to me that I should seek help from the medics, and as a result, it took weeks to recover my strength.

Running the Boston race had always been my dream, but the experience turned out to be one of the biggest disappointments on my marathon. Don't wait for hindsight to teach you the things you need to know about the particular marathon you're running. Find out the differences and how they can impact your race, and use your wisdom to prevent surprises and disappointments.

Exercise

Using the table below, write down the factors which influence your previous marathon and your current one. How are they different? What accommodations or special considerations will you need in training to prepare yourself for them?

Previous Marathon Conditions	Current Marathon Conditions	Training / Preparation Changes

mile
eight

Be Present

"Health is a large word. It embraces not the body only, but the mind and spirit as well... and not today's pain or pleasure alone, but the whole being and outlook of a man."

James H. West

Life is a routine. You get up in the morning and prepare for your scheduled daily responsibilities. After some time, the routine you've developed becomes quite comfortable. It's familiar, and you don't question it—until something happens that forces you to look it square in the eye and realize that maybe it isn't working after all.

By following your routine, you create repetition that helps you to fine-tune your routine. You carve out a beaten path to speed up your marathon. It's efficient and faster. You're focused because you know precisely what you're going to do next. But does your routine hum along at the expense of something else? Has your routine become so predictable that it doesn't allow you time for anything out of the ordinary? Or, worse yet, are you sacrificing things that are important to you as you follow the pattern you've created for your daily life?

The problem with routines is that while they do help us accomplish the duties and responsibilities we're charged with, they allow time for little else. Then, we become servants to our routines, making them the focal part of our existence, while neglecting to tend to other areas of our lives. Certainly, life becomes unbalanced when we're so focused on one thing that we take everything else for granted until it's too late. From experience, I can tell you that some things are not worth the sacrifice. Avoid becoming a slave to your routine by being present only to carry it out. Make sure you are present in your life for yourself and for others. Have dinner with your children. Call the friend you haven't caught up with in a while. Get to the gym and give your body the conditioning it demands. Reintroduce yourself to entertainment. Read something that feeds your mind with something new. Go see your dad. Because if you don't, life finds a way to tell you that you should.

My wake-up call came in 1979 during the Tehran hostage crisis. My life's marathon included military service, and I was proud to serve my country in the Air Force. Stationed on Andersen Air Force Base in Guam, I was busy running a B-52 weapons squadron on high alert. I was working 12-hour days and comfortable in my routine. I had grown my hair out to the maximum 1 ¼ inches, cut back on my running, and as a result, had gained 35 pounds. Admittedly, I was running my routine, but I wasn't running my life.

"Mike, you've got a phone call," my staff sergeant said. "It's your father."

"Hey, Dad," I answered, puzzled that he would call on a weekday morning. This was out of the norm for him. Why wasn't he at school, doing what he loved, transforming high school boys into championship basketball players?

"Mike," he said, "I need you to listen...I've had a heart attack."

Those words will resonate with me forever. I was scared and shocked. Here was a man, 53 years old, with a passion for athletics like no one I'd ever known. He had devoted his life to his players, moving his young family from one Midwestern town to another to transform failing basketball teams into champions. I never thought I'd hear the words "heart attack" associated with him.

Suddenly, I realized that if I didn't make some important changes in my routine, I'd be having a heart attack when I was 53, too. It dawned on me that while I was so busy doing the things I was supposed to do, I'd neglected to do the things I should do. I'd let my body go and taken my family for granted. For the first time in a long time, I came to the realization that the things I did or did not do today would affect me down the road. This discovery inspired me to put on my running shoes and grab hold of my life. I cut my hair, picked up the pace of my marathon, and shed the extra weight.

My dad also grabbed hold of his life. He picked up his marathon, exercising himself, not just his teams, and gave up artery-clogging Illinois farm food. He came back with 90 percent of his heart and the knowledge that he had to be present for himself.

Sometimes, routines need to be changed, no matter how comfortable they are. We need to be present in all areas of our lives, not just in our routine. Thanks, Dad, for making me present, and thanks for staying with me on the marathon.

Exercise

Be present in all areas of your life. Step out of your routine. Do one thing each day to create balance in your life and to tend to the people and things which you've neglected. If necessary, alter your routine permanently or scrap it altogether and create a new one which addresses not only your everyday responsibilities, but your future health and well being. Review your routine every six months to see if further changes need to be made.

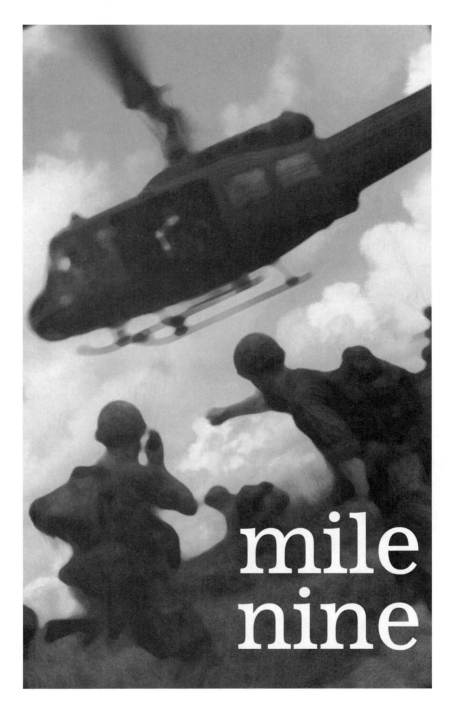

mile
nine

An Unpopular War

"How glorious it is - and also how painful - to be an exception."

Alfred de Musset

Your marathon is yours alone. No one else can run it for you. While you're busy running it, it can be easy to blend in with the crowd. You're moving forward, propelled by the momentum of thousands of others who are running their own marathons, too. But sometimes, when you step out of the marathon you're in, you become keenly aware that your marathon isn't the same as anyone else's, and you feel uncomfortable and desire to fit in again.

Standing out in a crowd can be a double-edged sword. Being unlike the norm can mean that you're exceptional in your marathon, or it can open the door to scrutiny and criticism from those who are running a different marathon. Blending in also has its advantages and disadvantages. It gives you a feeling of acceptance, but at the same time, can prevent you from being noticed. Neither is all good or all bad—it's how you adapt that ultimately will determine the outcome.

Blending in was not easy in 1971 for an Air Force Academy cadet looking for a fun night out on the town. The war in Viet Nam was raging, and so was the conflict here at home. The military was unpopular, and the controversy took a devastating toll on my class. When I arrived at the Academy on July 4, 1971, my class totaled 1,406. By the time we graduated, we were down to 756.

As freshmen, we were looking ahead at four long years which held a bleak outlook on the dating scene. Public opinion over the war would certainly spill over into our social lives. We could either accept that or do something about it. We chose the latter. Rather than opting to try to change the opinion of the majority, we needed a plan to help us blend in with society. There wasn't much we could do about our haircuts, but the uniforms – which were mandatory on and off base – had to go. This was one part of our marathon which would require conformity and stretching the rules.

So, I enlisted the aid of my cousin, Kathie, a junior at Colorado College, a small private, progressive liberal arts school in Colorado Springs. I got Kathie to agree to store our civilian clothes in her dorm room. We'd leave the academy, head to Kathie's, get changed and out we'd go. Without our uniforms, no one would be the wiser. Sure, there was risk involved, but we felt the rewards were well worth it.

The plan was working beautifully, and we were having a lot more fun on our marathons than the guys who wore their uniforms in town. Hurrying over to Kathie's, changing our clothes, and being civilians for a night became our standard operating procedure. Our plan was working without a hitch, until one Saturday night, when for a brief moment, it looked like it might not work.

I heard music as we approached her dorm room. I knocked on the door. Nothing. "Kathie," I called. The music stopped, but no one answered. "Kathie," I called again. Again, nothing.

"She's in there with her boyfriend," I explained. "Kathie!" I yelled, this time more urgently.

Finally, the dead bolt clicked and Kathie opened the

door. A guy in an open flannel shirt with shaggy hair and a mustache sat on the bed, grinning and shaking his head as we tumbled into the tiny room, intent on getting into our weekend outfits.

She and her boyfriend, whom she eventually married, waited in the hall while we transformed ourselves into civilians. "Thanks, Kath," I said, as we left her room, our uniforms neatly folded on her bureau. "We'll see you later."

We weren't about to give up our plan for anything or anyone. Not for my cousin's privacy or to avoid embarrassment. Blending in was all that mattered.

What matters to you? There are times when you'll choose to stand out in a crowd, and other times when you'll prefer to blend in. What you want is within your grasp, but you may have to bend the rules or concoct an unusual plan to make it happen. You might have to conform to popular opinion against your own wishes. Like me, sometimes you might have to make a few waves in someone else's life to blend in so you can make a wave of your own. Or, you might decide that it's your time to stand out and make a splash. Whatever your marathon brings, make a plan and keep going, adapting yourself to the uniqueness that surrounds you.

Remember, it's your marathon—only you can run it.

Exercise:

There will be times when your marathon is the popular route, and other times when it will go against the grain of popularity. Determine which route you want to follow and how you will uniquely adapt to the outside influences and environment along the way. How do you want to blend in, and how do you want to stand out? Make a plan and get going.

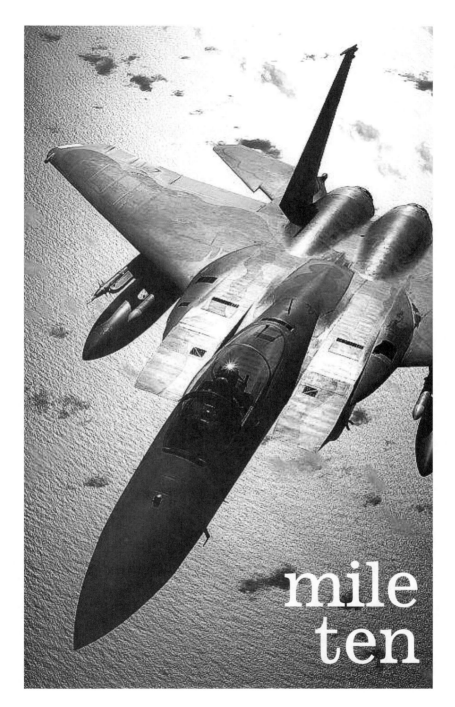

mile
ten

The Abyss

*"It is by going down into the abyss that we recover
the treasures of life.
Where you stumble, there lies your treasure."*

Joseph Campbell

Just as there will be times when you must conform or have a strong desire to excel, there will also be stretches of your marathon which will make you question your motives. You'll hit an impasse that feels like it cannot be crossed, or you might doubt your desire so much that you step back and contemplate if it's worth the effort. You may have reached the peak of your capacity, causing you to come to the realization that this marathon isn't suited for you at all. It's at that moment that German philosopher Friedrich Nietzsche states, "If you gaze long into an abyss, the abyss will gaze back into you."

An abyss has the ability to make you dig deep within yourself to determine if the marathon you're running is a good fit for you. Maybe you've reached your physical or mental endurance and just can't continue without taking a break. It might be that this particular marathon isn't meant to be a part of your journey. Maybe after beginning a marathon, you've made a self-discovery and came to that sudden a-ha moment that says, "I don't want to be here. I know it in my heart, in my head, and in my gut."

The point is your abyss will cause you to face your capacity and your uncertainties. It will make you turn inward and question your desire. When you do, you'll know whether the abyss will propel you to overcome your challenges or to avoid them altogether and choose a different path. You see, an abyss is an impasse which helps steer you in the right direction, even if it's an entirely different direction than the one you've traveled for years.

Think of your abyss as a lesson in self-discovery. Some might think of it as a reflection of themselves. It's telling you something, and when you face the reality of it, you'll learn a lot about yourself and what you really want in your marathon. My abyss caused me to come to a revelation which shocked not only myself, but also most everyone who knew me. It wasn't easy, but it taught me that I couldn't give my best unless I was totally honest with myself.

The roar of the T-37 jet trainer shattered the silence of the icy, clear sky over Enid, Oklahoma. I was in flight school and hurtling through the air at 400 miles per hour. As the aircraft banked to the left, I fought the sick feeling in my stomach. I swallowed over and over, white-knuckled and clenching the controls. I tried to ignore the nausea, concentrating on the speed and altitude indicators, the nose of the plane piercing the sky—anything to get past the fear that threatened to jeopardize my safety and my military career. It was freezing at 5,000 feet, but I was sweating, even my ankles were sweating. Finally, I came to the realization that it wasn't worth it. I knew in my head, my heart, and my queasy gut that this marathon was not for me.

"No more. If God wanted me to fly jets, I wouldn't be puking. I want out of the program. NOW." I never meant anything more definitively in my life.

I signaled to the Instructor Pilot to take over the controls before I turned away and vomited my breakfast. It was my third stint in the pilot's seat, and I was giving up.

I can't tell you how many people begged me to keep trying—my wing commander, my instructor pilot, my buddies. "This is the Air Force," they said. "You have perfect eyes. You don't join the Air Force to become a ground pounder. What will you do? Become a security policeman?"

What would I do? I didn't know. Up to that day, I had stepped up to every challenge that came my way on my marathon. For the first time, I was quitting. The "why" question was going to come up every day, and somehow, someway, I was going to have to find the answer to that question. Until then, I was stalled on my marathon.

You will face the abyss at some point, as well. When you do, you'll be required to face your own self truths, desires, and capacities. How will you respond? Will you be able to overcome the challenges and pull yourself up, or will you, like me, choose a marathon which is better suited for you?

mile
eleven

Build On Your Strengths

> "Leaders come in many forms,
> with many styles and diverse qualities.
> There are quiet leaders and
> leaders one can hear in the next county.
> Some find strength in eloquence,
> some in judgment,
> some in courage."
>
> **John Gardner**

Sometimes a marathoner needs to make a course correction. Whether the reason is within your control or you have no power over it, there are times when you need to step back and chart a new course. Saying you cannot continue on your present course is not a sign of weakness, but rather an acknowledgement of your strengths. It's an awakening that pulls you like a magnet toward your potential, instead of limiting you by keeping you on your current path.

When disappointment happens – especially when you disappoint yourself – you need to do an inventory of your strengths and make a course correction that builds on them. What do you do well? What building blocks have gotten you to this point? What gifts, talents, traits, or principles do you hold and honor which are unique and will attract success? This is no time to be modest, for modesty has a tendency to hide and stifle strengths, when you want to build on them.

I know that defining your strengths can be tough when you're discouraged. When things aren't working out the way you'd like them to, it's easy to kick yourself and lay the blame squarely in your own lap. But maybe, it's not your fault—perhaps the course you've been on is one that requires different strengths than the ones you have. This is actually a blessing, because now you know that changes are necessary and you have an opportunity to right your course and reveal your strengths, instead of fighting your weaknesses.

It's particularly daunting when you find that you need to make a correction on a course you've been on for a long time. Being a fighter pilot in the Air Force was my dream, and I'd invested a lot of time and energy in it. After spending four years at the Air Force Academy planning to fly fighter jets, learning that the maneuvers made me sick was disheartening, to say the least. I walked away from the course I'd been pursuing for so long, and for the first time in my life, I felt like a quitter. I was disappointed in myself and resigned myself to a dead-end military career. After all, it was unheard of and unthinkable that a member of the United States Air Force who had perfect vision would refuse to fly.

When I gave up flying, I had five years left to serve in the military. I had given up after just three tries. Instead of finding a new path which did suit me, I decided to coast through the one I was on for the next five years. But, I wasn't happy with the way everything had panned out, and it showed.

As people often do when they're not happy with themselves, I developed a negative attitude—one that hindered any potential progress I might have made. In reality, I became a wise guy who acted like I could skate through the next five years without applying myself or investing any extra effort, merely putting in my time. My weapons squadron assignment in Blytheville, Arkansas, wasn't what I'd signed up for, and my arrogance came across to everyone.

A few months into the assignment, I learned I had been bumped from officers' training.

"What's the deal?" I asked my superior officer.

"We don't need personnel with your attitude managing B-52s," he said. "This is serious stuff, and we need serious people."

That was my a-ha moment, when I suddenly realized that my attitude overpowered all of the strengths I had built over the years.

That was also the moment that I told myself, "Hey, I can't fly planes, but that doesn't mean that I don't have worthwhile skills, talents, and traits to offer the Air Force." Once I realized that it was in everyone's best interest if I focused on my strengths, instead of dwelling on my weakness, I committed to a new path. I began building on my education and my training, enrolled in graduate school, applied myself on the job and took my military career seriously. Eventually, I was promoted to assistant commander, running B-52 flight line squadrons at Anderson Air Force Base on Guam with 200 troops.

By building on my strengths, I was able to chart a different course and move forward. My experience in Guam gave me a strong foundation for the private sector, where I eventually earned the title of Marathon CEO. I'm certain that I wouldn't be where I am today if I had stayed stuck on my original course.

You see, biding your time doing something that isn't suited to you and your strengths is a route which won't get you anywhere. It will keep you stuck in your tracks, unhappily spinning your wheels. However, if you work with your strengths, you'll blaze your own course, and it will be one that motivates and inspires you to do the best you can in whatever marathon you run. You're not like anyone else—and shouldn't expect yourself to be. Break out of the cookie-cutter mode and build upon the unique strengths with which you've been blessed. Only then will you find your niche and reveal your full potential.

What are your strengths, and how can you use them differently to chart your own course?

mile
twelve

Bewildered

> "True stability results when presumed order and
> presumed disorder are balanced.
> A truly stable system expects the unexpected,
> is prepared to be disrupted,
> waits to be transformed."
>
> *Tom Robbins*

Everything is flowing at a smooth and even pace. You've mapped your route and made a plan, knowing exactly where you're going, content with the progress you've made. You're running along without a care in the world, and suddenly, the unexpected happens—you're injured, the stock market plummets, your company downsizes, or you lose a piece of your dream. The unexpected can throw you entirely off course, create delays, or disrupt your marathon. Sometimes, the only thing you can do when the unexpected happens is to accept it and deal with its effects after the fact.

Usually, though, the unexpected will leave you temporarily shocked and bewildered, wondering what just happened, and more importantly, why it happened to you. When you're young, the unexpected might be a nuisance, something that you want to put behind you as quickly as possible. Instead of facing it, there's a tendency to bury it and pretend it didn't happen. But, like it or not, the things you don't face now will still be there, silently lingering with you until you acknowledge and face them. As author David Corbin says in his book, *Illuminate: Harnessing the Positive Power of Negative Thinking*, "We can't solve everything we face, but we can't solve ANYTHING until we FACE it!" In other words, you can't move on until you've dealt with the unexpected things that happen in your life and accept the changes they've made to you and how they altered your path.

Of course, we try to prevent unwanted events in our lives. Sometimes, we can. Sometimes, we can even prepare for the unexpected so we can overcome it more easily. But sometimes, preparing for the unexpected is impossible and all you can do is react to it. I've learned the hard way that the unexpected cannot always be prevented and that the only thing you can do is face it and deal with its aftermath. Whether you choose to deal with it now or later is your choice, but you will have to face it at some point on your journey.

I walk through the cemetery, looking for a sign—a slight mound in the earth, the ghost of a tiny, rectangular outline. I find nothing. The heat shimmers, and the air hums with the sound of grasshoppers in the cotton fields that surround me. I stand alone, searching for what I thought I'd left in the past, but now realize will be with me for eternity.

Thirty years before...

I remember the ride too well. The limousine glided through Blytheville, as smooth and silent as a yacht slicing through swells in the water. The driver nosed its long, black, sleek bulk north, leaving behind the familiar civilization that had become a part of my home—the town hall, the fire department, the post office, the drug store, and the barber shop. We cruised through quiet residential streets shaded by stately elms. On each side were rows of neat bungalows and yards drinking from sprinklers shooting cool, delicate fountains across the summer grass. On any other day, I would have felt right at home, but not today. Not here, not now.

From the back seat, I stared blankly out the window, wishing away the presence of Father Bob who sat to my left, behind the driver. I didn't want to talk. I didn't want to feel. I only wanted to be somewhere else. Through it all, I was repeatedly haunted by the unanswered question: "What am I doing here?"

Three days before, Ryan's lifeless body had been taken from my wife's womb. She never saw him, but I did. I had to—hoping to find a physical sign of what went wrong, I held my firstborn and counted his fingers and his toes. To the naked eye, he was perfect. There wasn't any apparent reason why he was stillborn. There I was, crying and alone as I held our tiny four and ½ pound son, unprepared for the emotions or the trauma that his short presence in my life would create.

I didn't want to go through it. I didn't want to do this. If I'd had my way, I would have preferred to pretend it hadn't happened. Then, we could continue on with the happy, content lives we'd been living and act like the bottom hadn't fallen out from it. But as much as I wished I didn't have to, accompanying my baby and the tiny white casket I'd bought the day before was something I had to get through. Nobody knew where I was; my wife was at home, sedated and bewildered; my buddies were at work on the base. The driver, Father Bob, and I were alone on this sad journey—one which I wanted to put behind me as quickly as possible.

"No, I don't want a headstone," I told the undertaker. "No grave marker. Let's get this over with."

When we're young, we think we can bury the thing we don't want to face. We pretend it didn't happen. We move on. That's what I did, not knowing that I could run away from it for as long as I wanted, but it would always be with me, no matter how fast or far I ran. Later in my marathon, I discovered that it was still there—I hadn't put it behind me—I'd simply carried it *with me. Thirty years later, I returned, searching for the son I'd left behind and hoping to pay honor and tribute to him and the impact his short life had made on mine.*

There are things you cannot prevent, and unfortunately, things will happen in your life which you can't expect. When they do, don't try to ignore them and act like they were a temporary disruption, because the truth of the matter is, sometimes the unexpected shapes and transforms who we become. Good or bad, they mold us from the person we were into the person we will become. There are people and events which will stay with you forever. At some point in your marathon, you'll discover their presence and reflect on how it changed your path.

I couldn't find Ryan in the cemetery when I tried to locate him, but I know where he is and always has been...right here, with me.

I didn't choose this path, nor did I expect it. But that didn't keep it from transforming me and significantly impacting the man and father I've become. Ryan mattered.

mile
thirteen

Reach Out To Others

"The race advances only by the extra achievements of the individual. You are the individual."

Charles Towne

There will be miles on your marathon where you'll be called upon to stop, even if only for a moment, because a fellow marathoner needs a helping hand. We've all encountered people in need – the young mother with groceries and toddlers who needs a door opened, an out-of-work veteran who needs $5 for his next meal, a child who has fallen and needs a hug. Sometimes, people ask you for help, but more often it's something you do because you know it's right. Your heart leads the way; no request needed.

When you are asked to go out of your way to help someone in need, try not to think twice. The imprint left by your kindness is deeper and more lasting than the footprints you would have left if you'd continued without stopping. It might cost you a few dollars, or it might require you to take time out of an overfilled schedule. But the rewards will be worth it.

If the person who needs you is running along the same course as you, you probably won't think twice about slowing down, stepping aside, and offering assistance. These are the people you already know and love. But what about the people you don't know? You're passing by, lost in thought when you notice a woman struggling to get her wheelchair from the road to the sidewalk or an elderly man stymied by the self-checkout at the grocery store. You pause, wondering if someone else will appear to offer them aid. Do you really need to stop? Then, you wonder what would happen if you continued on, and no one offered any help. That's when you realize that your marathon isn't solely for your benefit.

I believe that even if our marathons follow different courses, we're all running together. Some of us might be on an easier portion than others, and some might be on a long and challenging incline. At some point, we all hit a rough spot and need someone to help us past it. I believe we're all still in the same race, and because of that, we have to look out for each other and help each other when the road gets rough. I could share with you a running story about when I needed help or when I stopped to lend a helping hand to a fellow marathoner, but instead I'll offer this touching true story about one small act of kindness that made all the difference in the life of a brave, vulnerable child..

The little girl stood frozen in the produce section, panic rising in her chest. She had planned everything so carefully. She had money in her pocket, $3 she found in her mother's vanity and $5 she got from her daddy the last time he'd come to visit. She'd made it across the field, and thankfully, there were no snakes in sight. She grabbed the handle of a grocery cart and walked through the automatic door, just like a grown-up.

But how do you pick out a cantaloupe?

She fought back tears, afraid that someone might notice her confusion. She didn't want anyone to know that Mother had been gone for days and the food in the apartment had run out. Her mother had been disappearing for a while now, ever since she'd left Daddy and moved with her daughter into an apartment near town.

"Aren't they beautiful?"

The gentle voice seemed to come out of nowhere. The little girl looked up to see a smiling woman. "Here, let me help you pick one out. You want it to be ripe. It should be heavy for its size and the spot at the top should give a little when you press on it."

"An angel," thought the little girl. She smiled in thanks and turned her cart away. She headed straight to the cashier, her cantaloupe in the cart with the crackers and peanut butter she'd already placed there. She paid for her groceries, made it back across the field and returned to the cool safety of her empty apartment. Everything would be fine, she thought happily. She'd have cantaloupe for supper and make peanut butter and crackers for lunch. Her second grade teacher wouldn't suspect a thing. And maybe, when she got home from school, Mother would be home again.

Every act of kindness, no matter how small, makes an impact on someone's life. Reach out to others on your marathon. Pick them up, help them past the rough spots, or carry them for a few steps. It might not seem that important to you, but it will influence someone else's life.

Today the little girl in the grocery store is a philanthropist who has dedicated countless hours to help others. She is forever grateful to the woman who came to her rescue at the cantaloupe display.

Exercise:

Write down one thing you did today to help someone else. How did it make you feel?

....

....

....

....

....

Now, make a conscious effort to do one thing, no matter how small, to help someone or give back to others.

mile
fourteen

Find Joy In Simple Things

"It is always the simple things that change our lives. And these things never happen when you are looking for them to happen. Life will reveal answers at the pace life wishes to do so.
You feel like running, but life is on a stroll."

Donald Miller

As you're busy running your life and your marathon, there is a tendency to become self-involved, focused on what you're doing and where you're going. Focus, determination, and concentration are great—but they can cause you to lose sight of the little things which are right in front of you. So often, these little things are simple—a butterfly, wildflowers, the playfulness of a puppy, a rainbow in the spring, a cool breeze on a hot summer day. Yes, these seem like small, everyday things, but they are also priceless gifts, rewarding you with their simplicity and delightful presence along your arduous journey. Sometimes, the unexpected joy found in the simplest things is a reminder that the world has amazing things to offer—if we can only pause long enough to see and appreciate them.

As you're running your marathon, you'll be blessed with sights and sounds that will make your run a much more enjoyable one. Revel in them—note the splendid color of the landscape where it meets the sky, the scent of fresh lilacs, and the laughter of children at play. Allow yourself to experience what is going on around you and take advantage of the opportunity to see the world through fresh, new eyes. When you do, you'll give yourself endless reasons to smile and be content in your world.

As we grow older and assume more responsibilities, we lose touch with the world around us and forget how to experience joy in the simple things life offers. You might find yourself more concerned with material things, so focused on taking care of your car, house, or business that you don't have time to enjoy any of them. Or in a runner's world, you might be so focused on your pace, speed, and time that you forget to enjoy the sights and sounds during your run. Don't become so intense in your marathon that you lose sight of the small, but oh-so-pleasant joys along the way.

Sadly, some people don't heed this message until something happens which profoundly changes their life, like being diagnosed with an illness. Only then do they stop and admire the beauty of nature, take a moment to enjoy petting a friendly pup, or to do nothing but sit back and relax on a warm summer day. It is then that they realize that there is more to life than chasing the almighty dollar—realizing, in fact, the life they've been living wasn't bad at all once they took the time to enjoy it.

Do you remember when you were a child and thought dandelions were beautiful? How about the magic in finding a four-leaf clover or the amazement in watching a seed grow into a plant or a tree? There was joy in something as simple as being splashed with cool water on a hot summer afternoon or watching the first snowfall. Then something happened and we were all given the huge gift of responsibility and no longer had the time to relish in the wonder of these little joys. But we should.

On the streets of Sondrio, Italy, a group of young adults were on a mission. Armed with signs that said "FREE HUGS" in several different languages, they walked along busy streets and storefronts to offer just that—free hugs to anyone and everyone. At first, people kept walking, not wanting to stop whatever they were doing or skeptical about hugging a stranger. These young men and women weren't discouraged, though. They proudly held their signs over their heads for all to see as they approached passersby. Eventually, they got one hug, then another and another. The hugs became more frequent as people stopped to watch others walk up for their free hug. They hugged men and women, children, teenagers, senior citizens, and musicians, and as they did, the joy with each encounter was evident. Everyone who got their arms wrapped around them wore a smile, some walked away with a dance in their step. Onlookers admired the show, stopping to take pictures before taking their turn. Some people even ran into a big bear hug, while others preferred a group hug. But the one thing that was consistent throughout every encounter was that it brought visible joy to the lives of everyone—the hugger, the person being hugged, and the people who paused to witness strangers come together and touch each other.

This mission was videotaped, and the following quote by Oscar Wilde ended the video: "For one moment our lives met, our souls touched." And it was all because of something as simple, as powerful, and as joyful as a hug.

A gentleman by the name of Juan Mann started the Free Hugs campaign in a desire to spread joy, even if only for a moment. The Free Hugs campaign is now global and has provided millions of smiles and touched the lives of those giving and receiving one of the simplest things in life—a hug.

There's joy all around us in this busy marathon of life. Stop for a moment and enjoy the simple things—smell the roses and take a few seconds out of your day to hug and be hugged. Your marathon is too short to deprive yourself of it.

Exercise:

At the end of the day, make a list of all of the things, no matter how small, that brought you joy today. Tomorrow, specifically look for small things that make your marathon more enjoyable and allow yourself to share them with others along the way.

mile
fifteen

Meet A Princess

"Laugh at yourself first, before anyone else can."

Elsa Maxwell

While there is joy to be found in your marathon, there will also be a few mile markers that you'd like to erase. Everyone has them—those moments when you make a mistake and wish you could hide under the covers until everything blows over. Hiding from life rarely accomplishes anything, however. I've found that the best you can do is to save face and limit the damage.

You know what I'm talking about; you slip and almost fall, doing a comedic balancing act that you're sure everyone in the world witnessed. The seat of your pants rips out, you trip in front of strangers or admiring fans, you open your mouth and insert your foot...Yes, these are all part of your marathon. While you find them humiliating and embarrassing, you're also worried about what everybody else is thinking about your mishap—are they laughing at you, muttering something about how clumsy you must be, or are they feeling sorry for you for your blunder?

Well, I've had those experiences, and I've learned that it's not how you fall that matters, but more importantly, how you pick yourself up. Too often, we tend to take ourselves too seriously, putting unnecessary importance on things that matter only to us. Most of the time, when you lose grace, you're the only one who is going to dwell on it and remember it; the only time other people place a great deal of importance on it is when you do.

So, those times when you fall from grace and get red in the face call for you to gracefully pick yourself up and dust yourself off, without placing any undue attention to the matter. Instead of overstressing and over exaggerating what happened, do just the opposite—make light of it. That will encourage other people to do just the same. It's true that everything is viewed from an entirely different perspective when people laugh with you, instead of at you.

Now, if there's ever an occasion when gracefulness and composure are protocol, it's when you are in elite company—in the presence of royalty. You don't want to do anything that would cause unnecessary attention toward yourself, especially if it's negative attention. I enthusiastically welcomed my first opportunity to meet royalty in London. My company was the marathon event sponsor, and I held the esteemed position as captain of the corporate running team. What a great place to run in a marathon, I thought, as I was swept up in the rich history which surrounded me.

Indeed, it was spectacular. The gala fund-raiser was scheduled for that evening, the night before the race. Months of preparation had gone into making it an elaborate and memorable international event. Princess Diana would be attending, and I would be privileged to be introduced to her. I still couldn't believe it.

Among my rituals the day before a marathon is to go for a short, leisurely run. As I left my hotel in the afternoon, I soaked up the energy of the city. Running along the crowded, busy streets, I thought about the coming events. Would Princess Diana be as beautiful in person as she was in photographs? What would I say to her? I was so looking forward to it and enjoying the sights that my mind was far away from what I was doing.

On my way back to the hotel, I passed a group of sight-seers who were lined up for a bus tour. I should have been watching where I was going, but in my euphoria, I gave them a big, cheerful wave...they were all looking at me as I ran head first into a decorative, historic, iron, hard-as-steel post.

I heard the smack and saw stars. Oh, the sound. Oh, the pain.

I grabbed my injured head and reeled back toward the crowd. Looking around in a daze, I saw the amazement, the horror, and yes, the amusement, on the faces of the people I'd just greeted.

"Not a problem, nothing to worry about," I shouted, hiding my humiliation and embarrassment with a grin. "I'll be fine."

In a marathon, you keep going forward. That's what I did, until I got into my room and held a cold wet cloth to my throbbing head while calling room service for some much-needed ice to soothe my wounds.

That evening when the gala started, the right side of my face was a spectacular shade of purple. As I approached Princess Diana in the receiving line, I admired how graciously she greeted each guest with a warm smile. Then it was my turn. As she turned to greet me, her eyes widened momentarily before she regained her poise.

"You should see the other guy," I said.

The next day, I went out and ran a marathon.

By making light of the situation, I saved myself the embarrassment of having to explain the circumstances behind my injury. Instead of looking at my misfortune as a reason to pity myself and hide under the covers, I chose to laugh at myself and find humor in the situation. From that point on, I could move past it and act like it had never happened.

When you run into a post, how will you react? Will you be too embarrassed to face the world, or will you step forward and keep moving? The damage is done, but you have a unique opportunity to pick yourself up gracefully and still be worthy of keeping company with a princess. Don't take your marathon too seriously—laugh at yourself so others will laugh with you, instead of at you.

mile
sixteen

Hit the Walls and Reach New Heights

"Having hit a wall, the next logical step is not to bang our heads against it."

Stephen Harper

Just as I did when I ran into that iron post in London, there are times when you're going to hit a wall. It's a point in time when you feel like you've gone as far as you can possibly go, whether the circumstances are within your control or not. In running a marathon, hitting the wall is when the muscle energy stored in the body is depleted, so the body has to turn to fat as a source of metabolism. In life, it's a point where you come to an impasse that's preventing any progress, stopping you dead in your tracks. Whether you run into a post or hit the glass ceiling, you now have to find a way to go around it or break through the limitations before you.

Women are all too familiar with hitting a glass ceiling in their careers, and the phenomenon also applies to other circumstances. In some industries or careers, you can only go so high before you need further training, education, or experience to climb any higher. People hit the wall in other ways, too. An individual attempting to lose weight through diet and exercise hits a plateau; a person trying to enter a non-traditional career for their age or sex can hit the wall. A runner striving to increase speed or break a personal record can hit the wall, feeling that they have reached the limit of their capabilities.

But, hitting the wall is often an internal belief—a lack of confidence in yourself that you can overcome and find the determination, motivation, or that something extra that will help you jump the hurdle in front of you. It's a test of your will and your desire—how much do you want this and are you willing to do whatever it takes to make it happen, despite the odds?

Sherri Cothrun has hit walls. At critical stages of her marathon, starting in high school, influential people threw roadblocks in her path. "Surely, you mean legal secretary," her high school counselor replied when Sherri said she planned to be a lawyer.

Women of Sherri's generation were not expected to be lawyers. Their career options were usually limited to teaching, nursing, or secretarial work. But Sherri didn't let that stop her from pursuing her dream career. Instead of falling victim to the walls and changing her expectations to accommodate society, she took lessons from them. "Every step just prepared me for the next gender bias," she said. "Every lesson forged the way for the next."

Today, she is a family lawyer with almost three decades of practice behind her. By using the knowledge and insights she gained on both her marathons – as a lawyer and as a stepmother – Sherri has enhanced the contributions she makes in both roles. Her experience working with troubled families prepared her for the rigors of a being a stepparent – and made her better at it – and her experience as a stepparent has given her empathy for and insight into her clients' situations that make her a better family law attorney. She understands how children feel when their families are breaking apart.

Sherri has always believed that gender should never prevent a man or woman from pursuing a dream...or even a learning opportunity. Here are some of the walls she has hit on her marathon:

The high school policy in Yuma, Arizona, that barred girls from shop class. "I wanted to be self-sufficient, to learn how to use tools, power tools," she says. She got special dispensation from the principal.

Disapproval from teachers and classmates at the New Mexico Military Institute when she became the first girl to be admitted. Instead of being intimidated, she took college-level courses that landed her as a second semester sophomore at New Mexico State.

Her father's news about two weeks before starting at New Mexico State that there was no money for dorm living. She'd been an honorary member of the New Mexico State Board of Education and got the chairman to intervene (after the deadline) to get a student loan.

More disapproval, this time from law school professors at Pepperdine University, who suspected she was there to hunt for a husband.

Skeptical employers who thought she wasn't serious about her career. "We invest in our associates, and we don't think you're here to stay," they said, after she drove herself from Los Angeles to Houston and passed the Texas bar exam.

Finally getting a job and not liking it. "I was doing what I wanted to do for half my life, and it turned out like this," she says. "I realized every law firm would be like that. I wouldn't have control over what I did. I would have to deal with politics."

Less than two years out of law school, Sherri went solo into private practice. Family law became her specialty. "I could connect with people," she says. "I really cared about them. I felt like I was really helping people, even if only by making their divorce less stressful. It's what I came into law for."

About 10 years later, Sherri hit the wall again. Representing a father seeking custody of his three children was an uphill battle since the courts usually sided with the mother, but Sherri won the case after sharing information about the mother's clinical depression. As she left the court and reached her car she felt sick. "How in the world can this family recover from this?" she thought. "There's just got to be another way."

Today, she helps families avoid the trauma of the courts by acting as a mediator who helps people reach their own agreements instead of going before a judge. "I tell them that this is the opportunity for them to take responsibility for their own children," she says.

Sherri hit a lot of walls. But she found a way to circumvent each of them and took responsibility for her outcomes, rather than letting the walls control them. She was fortunate that her parents never put limits on her because she was a girl. And at each wall she found a teacher, a friend or a mentor who helped her over. You, too, can look at each wall which pops up along your path as an opportunity to accept responsibility for your life and accomplishments. Rather than looking at the wall and turning back, do whatever it takes to move it, go around it, or climb over it. Don't accept less than what you deserve, and don't give less than what you truly want for yourself.

Everybody hits a wall, but it's those who don't let it stop them that cross the finish line.

Exercise:

What walls are you currently facing in your marathon?

....

....

....

....

Name three things you can do to break through or climb over
those walls:

1. ....

....

....

2. ....

....

....

3. ....

....

....

Now, get moving!

mile
seventeen

Choose To Respond

"Don't dwell on what went wrong.
Instead, focus on what to do next.
Spend your energies on moving forward
toward finding the answer."

Denis Waitley

In your marathon, you'll encounter things over which you have no power. Your computer freezes in the middle of an important project. Your cell phone drops calls or you lose service when you need it most. It rains on your parade or your picnic. These are all things over which you have no control. Sure, they're frustrating. We don't like to feel powerless, so when problems arise, we tend to become angry and vent our frustrations, cursing our computer, Mother Nature, or our darn undependable phone.

How often does that happen to you? How many times have you wanted to slam your computer onto the floor? Machines and technology have a way of doing that to us because we're at their mercy. But if you were to act out your frustrations, what would it solve? Nothing—you'd simply create another problem. Your cell phone would be lying in a ditch somewhere and your computer would be doing its part to fill the local landfill. Now, you have an entirely different problem.

Rather than reacting to your problem, why not try another tactic and respond to it? After all, that is the only thing you can control. You can't control the problem, but you can control your response. Often, the way you respond determines your outcome. Henry Ford stated it well: "Don't find fault, find a remedy." Instead of placing blame, take an honest assessment of the problem and determine what you can do now to minimize the damage or solve it.

It's been said that it's not the size of our problem that is important, but rather our response to it. Often, that's what sets great leaders apart from the rest—their ability to assess a problem objectively and respond to it in the same way.

I was winding up a 10-day road trip and had arrived at Houston's Hobby Airport at 11:30 on a Friday night. It had been a long week, and in addition to being really tired, my titanium hip was aching. I wanted nothing more than to get home.

When I got to the parking lot, I squeezed the keypad to unlock my car.

"Hmm, don't the lights usually come on?" I thought. "That's weird."

Did I tell you I was really tired? That it hurt my head to think? I looked at the car for a while and finally my brain kicked in. "There is no power. There is no power in the freaking car…"

Moments like these trigger your reactive state; you want to let loose your fury and frustration. These are the times when you forget that the event is only 10 percent of the equation and that the 90 percent – your response – is what really counts. That's when we let our emotions get the better of us.

Here was my emotional reaction. "The battery is dead. I just paid $1,700 to get this car fixed. I want to break the window. Why me?"

Yes, I wanted to scream, kick, or put my fist through the window. But internally, I knew that wasn't going to help the situation. If anything, it was only going to make a bad situation worse. So, I chose to respond in a rational manner.

"I'll take my cell phone out of my pocket and call a taxi. I'll call my mechanic in the morning and have him take care of this."

That's precisely what I did.

Have you ever seen two people react differently to the very same thing? One gets upset, and rants and raves to the point where they can be heard in the next zip code. The other takes a deep breath, contemplates their situation in a calm, rational manner, and chooses a constructive response. Within a short time, the rational person has made progress toward solving the problem, while the emotional person hasn't even begun to deal with it.

Remember that the event – the computer crashing, the dropped call on the cell phone, the dead car battery – is only 10 percent of the equation. It's your response, not your reaction, that sees you through. Your reaction will serve no worthwhile purpose—your response, however, is the first step toward constructively solving the problem. My instinct was to react, to break the freaking window, but instead I chose to respond, to keep going...and I got home.

There are some things over which you have no control. However, you can always control your response to them. The power's in your hands. Use it to move forward, rather than allowing it to hold you back.

mile
eighteen

Set Goals

*"If you want to live a happy life, tie it to a goal,
not to people or things."*

Albert Einstein

When I found my car, albeit without power, in the airport parking lot, my short-term goal was to get home, and as quickly as possible. My long-term goal in that situation was naturally to return power to the automobile so I could rely on it when I needed it. Two different goals—each attainable, but in different ways and at different times. Everything in life presents goals—trimming an inch from your waistline to running a marathon, writing a term paper to completing a degree, saving a down payment for a house to building a nest egg for retirement. But, your progress toward accomplishing any of those things will be dim if you don't have a goal and a time frame established to achieve it.

Bestselling author and founder of the Science of Success principles Napoleon Hill said, "A goal is a dream with a deadline." When you state that dream and give it a deadline, you're far more likely to achieve it than someone who simply wishes it to happen. Wishes leave your dream up to the undependable factor of luck, and as we all know, the stories of success based on chance are few and far between. But, when you set a goal, you have a bull's eye within sight to aim for and aspire to hit, motivating you and keeping you focused on the end result.

It's also true that people who set goals tend to be happier. They accomplish more because they stay on track as they progress toward successfully achieving the things they want in life. With each accomplishment, they become more confident and inspired to do more, so they set another goal, and then yet another, each bringing them more growth, success, and satisfaction in their life.

Have you ever felt like you're spinning your wheels and getting nowhere? That every day is the same as the day before, with a lot of work but no real measurable progress? If that sounds like you, try setting a goal. What is it that you want to accomplish? Do you want to feel the thrill and the internal victory of running a half or full marathon? Maybe you've always wanted to start your own business, learn another language, start a new hobby, or tackle (and complete) a big project. Starting today, do something to make that happen—set a goal and give it a deadline.

Your dream is your long-term goal; each of the steps you have to take to accomplish it are the short-term goals that, when met, will keep you on track and propel you closer to achieving it. It's the best way to make wishes come true.

In life and work, Larry Lichnovsky has kept on track by setting goals—lots of them. When he reaches a goal, he sets a new one, always in pursuit of what's ahead for him as he maps out his life. He's operated businesses, made them successful, and then sold them. Each goal prepared him for the next, providing him with the confidence, determination, and perseverance to do more and be more.

Larry also runs marathons—lots of them. In 2009, he crossed the finish line next to Vermont's scenic Lake Champlain. It was a clear, windless, 23-degree day, and he'd reached one of his highest goals—running a marathon in all 50 states in the nation.

"When I started this, I had two passions," he said. "I enjoy traveling, and I enjoy running the marathon and the challenge that comes with it."

Having run races in all 50 states, Larry has set a new goal to run in 100 marathons before his 70th birthday in 2018...maybe on every continent.

"It's only a thought right now," he said. "This is how things start. You start by thinking about it."

He trains four days a week, running 50 to 60 miles, sometimes solo, sometimes enjoying the camaraderie of others. His next marathon will be between the surf and the mountains in California's Big Sur region. He's working toward his goal all of the time, knowing the internal satisfaction that comes from turning a goal into a reality.

If Larry hadn't set goals, it's likely that he wouldn't have reaped so many rewards. But like so many others, he knows that a dream isn't something left to chance and that the responsibility to make it happen is totally his. He's proof that in business and in life, we can accomplish what we want, as long as we define what our goals are and take action to make them happen.

What if your goal, though, is a lofty one? Maybe you want to run a marathon, but you're not a runner—you haven't even run around the block. How do you set about accomplishing such a big goal? You set smaller goals within the long-term goal. You might be overwhelmed at the prospect of actually running 26.2 miles, thinking it's not achievable. That's when you break your goal into smaller goals that are more easily achieved, like running a quarter of a mile, walking, and then running another quarter of a mile. When you've met that goal, you move forward to the next, running a half mile before stopping, then a mile, and so on. Each goal is an accomplishment that helps you to meet the larger goal. Before you know it, you'll be running a half or full marathon, something that you might have thought impossible not too long ago.

So, now it's your turn. It's never too early or too late to make your dreams come true, and a goal will get you there faster and easier than you ever thought possible.

Exercise:

In the exercise on the following page, you have an opportunity to define what you really want to accomplish. Then, you'll break down your goals into smaller, short-term goals that will get you there.

A. *Business/Career Goal*

My goal is. ....

....

Deadline: ....

Short-Term Goals:

1. ....

....

    Deadline: ....

2. ....

....

    Deadline: ....

3. ....

....

    Deadline: ....

B.   *Personal Goal (Fitness, Health, Finances, Hobbies, etc.)*

My goal is: ....

....

Deadline: ....

Short-Term Goals:

1. ....

....

   Deadline: ....

2. ....

....

   Deadline:...

3. ....

....

   Deadline: ....

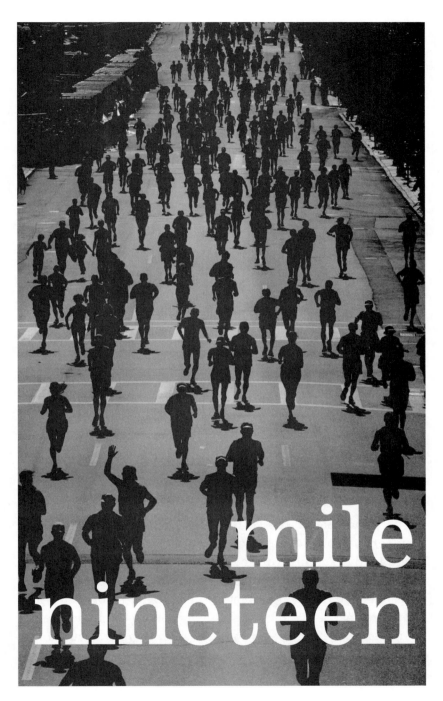

mile nineteen

Learn from Others

"Wise men learn by other men's mistakes,
fools by their own."

Proverb

Life is a miracle. We are born knowing how to do two things—eat and breathe. Nobody has to teach us those things; they are survival instincts built-in at birth. Everything else, though, has to be learned. We have to learn to sit, crawl, walk, talk, read, write, and count, among thousands of other things that we are taught by others. Those are all important skills we need to succeed in life; yet, are they the only lessons available that can impact not only our success, but our survival? I don't think they are.

Other people can teach you so much! From basic life skills to work skills, they offer their wisdom and experience to your efforts throughout your life. In reality, learning from others is the least expensive education you can receive, but also as good as, if not better than, any degree. In fact, there are things that you can learn from others that cannot be taught as well in a book or class.

Who teaches these things? Potentially everyone, everywhere. A homeless man on a street corner might teach you humility. By example, your next-door-neighbor might reveal to you the benefits of sharing and lending a helping hand. A major league ball team might teach you the benefits of teamwork. There are coaches who can teach you how to improve or excel in sports, leadership, goals, and life. And, there are your family and friends who teach you the joys and benefits of kindness, friendship, and love.

Some of these people teach these things intentionally, some merely by observation. For example, I learned from my father's heart problems to take care of my own health. But, he wasn't the only one who taught me that some of the greatest lessons I'll ever receive are by example. Tony was another man who taught me a lesson I'll never forget, and in doing so, he encouraged me to share his story so others can also learn from him.

Tony was everyone's go-to guy, and he played many roles. He was a father, grandfather, scout troop leader, and a member of the church choir. As operations engineer for our company, WFI Southwest LP, he was a busy and popular man, constantly sought out for his excellent advice. He was there for everybody. The only person Tony neglected was himself.

Every day, his Corolla would groan and sway as he hefted his 300-pound frame out of the driver's seat. Just walking from his car to his office was a laborious task, leaving him breathless by the time he got to his desk. Once he got there, though, Tony worked longer hours than anyone, often until 10 p.m. He was pushing himself to the brink—literally—and it was obviously taking its toll on him.

This was how Tony's life continued, until he suddenly suffered a long series of strokes. He was no longer able to work, and his coworkers missed him terribly. As the costs for his medical care rose, so too did the company's health insurance premiums—by 125 percent.

Four months after the onset of his illness, Tony came to the company holiday party, his frame shrunken to a mere 145 pounds. He had lost more than half of his body weight and looked nothing like the Tony we had known and loved. From his wheelchair, he asked for the microphone. If knowing Tony's health woes and seeing him so frail and ill hadn't taught us anything, his words certainly did.

"Please take care of yourself first," he said. "Otherwise, you won't be able to help others. Learn from what happened to me."

A few months later, at the age of 59, Tony, our good friend and coworker, died. His marathon was over.

Sometimes, the person who is dying shares life's most important lessons. They are able to look back on their life and priorities and see them from a different perspective. Nobody who is at the end of their journey wishes they'd spent more time at work—they usually wish they'd taken better care of themselves, enjoyed the small things more often, and taken the opportunity to do the things they'd always wanted, but had put off until someday. Well, for people like Tony, sometimes someday doesn't come.

My primary emotions were grief and guilt. I was overcome with grief because I had lost a good friend and a great contributor to the company—in many ways, he was irreplaceable. I also felt guilty because I could have and should have done more. Maybe I should have spoken up and told Tony I was worried about his health and his weight. I could have encouraged him to start a fitness program or tried to coax him away from his desk more often. I didn't do those things, but I did learn from what happened to Tony. Maybe that was Tony's legacy to all of us.

Shortly after, I met with my CFO, who was 80 pounds overweight, and convinced him to get a complete checkup. He reluctantly agreed. The tests revealed polyps, and within six months, he managed to get his weight down from 263 to 190 pounds. Had it not been for Tony, I probably would not have pushed him to get tested. Had it not been for Tony, I might have made the same mistake twice.

Yes, other people can teach you so much. Everyone sought advice from Tony on a daily basis, but it was his life and six simple words that made the greatest impact: "Learn from what happened to me." Learn from Tony and the people in your life so you don't make the same mistakes, especially ones that can shorten your marathon or make it less enjoyable.

On our marathon, we take a great deal for granted, and that includes life. Other people can teach us a lot—if we keep our eyes open.

mile twenty

Encourage
and Teach Others

"A teacher affects eternity. No one can tell where his influence stops."

Henry Adams

I learned a lot from Tony's tragic experience, and I pass on the lesson he taught to me whenever I can. In telling me to learn from his illness, he was hoping to make a positive impact on my life. What he didn't know was that he helped me to become a teacher. I use Tony's story to encourage others to make conscious, healthy decisions and to change their marathons for the better.

We've all had teachers who have influenced us. There was the teacher who ignited your interest in world history, the teacher who went the extra mile to tutor you through the rough spots in algebra. Coaches taught you valuable lessons, and mentors taught you how to make good decisions. Once students themselves, teachers share their unique knowledge, skills, and experience to help you along your marathon.

Reversing your role from student to teacher is one way you can make a profound difference in someone else's marathon, as well as your own. It's a well-known fact that teachers don't choose their careers for the money. Instead, they have a strong desire to make a difference in the lives of others. You, too, can be a teacher by sharing your own experiences, insights, or knowledge with others. You, too, can help them learn, grow, and pursue their passion. Teaching may be one of the most deeply rewarding things you can ever do.

After years of working in the corporate sector, I longed to do something more rewarding. Ultimately, I set out to teach others the leadership skills I'd learned. Teaching people to become marathon fit by making conscious choices in their lives is the most enriching and satisfying thing I've done in my career. Making a difference in other people's lives has made a profound difference in mine.

Jane Luco has made a difference in thousands of lives. For 30 years, she has inspired others to reach farther, push harder, and dig deeper. "It ain't walkin' the dog," she says, to the amusement of the sweating crowd in the church gymnasium. They've heard it dozens of times before, but they still smile as they join the thousands of Houstonians who have relied on Jane to become physically fit and feel better about themselves.

Since 1980, when she started her Jazzercise franchise, Jane has taught upwards of 16,000 classes to thousands of women (and a few men). Today, she finds herself teaching the daughters of her early students, sometimes in mother-daughter teams.

"When I started this, nobody knew what it was," she says. "Who knew?"

Year after year, her students come trudging through the parking lot, pulling wheel bags stuffed with weights, towels, gym mats, and water bottles. There is no laundry service at this gym and no fancy high-end juice bar. But there is Jane, always at the door to say welcome, always eager to encourage and inspire them to leave their comfort zones.

She teaches from a ten by six foot stage built on wheels by her husband Jerry. There are no mirrors on the walls. The electric fans were donated by an appreciative student. Sometimes the church staff forgets to turn on the AC ahead of time.

But the students keep coming – 50 to 75 to every class – and each year the numbers grow.

Jane grew up in West, a small central Texas town north of Waco, the youngest of five children, and started working in her grandparent's restaurant – Sulak's – when she was in eighth grade. The whole family – brothers, sisters, aunts and uncles – were there, cleaning, waiting on tables, sassing the customers and pooling their tips. The business was open seven days a week from five in the morning to 11 or 12 at night.

She graduated from the University of Texas with all A's – it was expected – and eventually moved to Houston to start one of the city's first Jazzercise classes. With few fitness options in those days, she was overrun with business and had to set up a waiting list.

The fitness craze boomed a couple of years later and competition became fierce. Jane Fonda tapes were on sale everywhere. It seemed like an aerobics studio was opening on every street corner. Swanky, multi-story gyms with chrome, track lighting, pounding music, hot tubs, saunas, towels and hair dryers offered special membership rates.

But the students kept coming. Even when she was evicted from the YWCA (they thought they could make money running their own aerobics classes). Even when she landed in a scary neighborhood.

Today, most of the swanky gyms and aerobics studios have closed their doors. Hot Yoga is fizzling, Tai Bo has come and gone, and Jane Fonda's methods were long ago alleged to be dangerous to the knees.

Yet, Jane is going strong. She continues to greet her students – day after day, week after week, year after year – as they come through the church gym door. She knows their names; she knows the names of their kids, and she knows when they miss class. On their birthdays, she lets them pick the music and invites them to dance with her on stage.

She urges them to stretch further to challenge their cores, to hop higher to build bone density, and to use heavier weights to build muscle. She'll stay behind to explain the subtleties of a grapevine, a toe-ball-heel, or a jazz square.

At least five times a year, class members carry tables and chairs from the church meeting room and sit down to the homemade cooking from Jerry—chili, gumbo, eggs migas, and salsa. Students bring side dishes – deviled eggs, tamales, corn bread, and watermelon – the professional baker in the back row brings chocolate cupcakes with creamy chocolate icing.

"In the restaurant business, in a family business, you don't just go to work. You go above and beyond to be with that customer," she says. "I'm motivated because I truly enjoy doing it. I truly enjoy being around these people."

Jane is proof that when you love what you do and you share it with others, you become a real leader in your industry and your community. As William Ward once said, "The mediocre teacher tells. The good teacher explains. The superior teacher demonstrates. The great teacher inspires."

Inspire someone today—teach them how they can make their marathon a better one. In return, yours will be, too.

mile
twenty
one

There's Good News and Bad...

"The bad news is time flies.
The good news is you're the pilot."

Michael Althsuler

Life's unexpected moments throw curves into your marathon, sometimes delaying your run, and sometimes throwing you off course completely. Those are defining moments, and the way you respond to them can ultimately determine your outcome and your future.

We've all heard someone say, "I have good news, and I have bad news." We usually delight in the good news and are eager to hear it; on the flip side, we cringe with the bad news and bemoan its arrival. Good news by itself is a cause for celebration. Bad news, on the other hand, we prefer to do without. Who wouldn't? But when the good news and the bad news come at the same time, it leaves us with mixed feelings—uncertain how to react. Which one takes priority in our minds? It's usually the bad news; however, it is possible that the two can balance each other, making the good news less celebratory, but the bad news less devastating.

Let me throw another possibility your way. Can being the recipient of bad news actually be a good thing? Sure, it may not seem like it at the moment that you receive it, but later, is it possible that you'll look back on it and see that while it was not welcome at the time, it became a blessing down the road?

It caused you to alter your course and regain your footing, but when you did, you found that your marathon was more rewarding and enjoyable than ever before. Well, that's precisely what happened to me when I heard, "Mike, I've got good news, and I've got bad news..."

The acquisition of ADT was rumored, but I wasn't worried about my job. In fact, I was confident and secure that I wasn't going anywhere. I was the go-to guy for business turnarounds; for a dozen years, I'd made top performers out of failing operations. The success I'd experienced had a downfall, though, as I moved from one company to another, uprooting my family over and over again because that's what ADT asked me to do. We'd changed addresses plenty of times: Milwaukee, Cincinnati, New York City, and Hartford. From there, we moved to Atlanta and called it home. The company chairman liked me so much he'd nicknamed me the "Marathon CEO." So, as you can see, I didn't think my job was in jeopardy. I was one of the 'safe' ones.

When I got to work that fateful morning, Tony Esposito, VP of Human Resources and friend—who should have been in his own office in Boca Raton—was waiting for me. "Here's the good news, Mike," he said. "Wall Street loves the possible acquisition prospects, and our stock is soaring."

Wow, that's great, I thought. Yet, there was something nagging in the back of my mind. When you hear, "Here's the good news," inevitably, you wait for the other shoe to drop. It did.

"And here's the bad news. You're not going to be part of the new company. There's no chair for you at the table."

Talk about an unexpected moment. I didn't even see it coming, yet suddenly, here I was speechless...and unemployed.

The next thing I knew, security was walking me out the door. In a matter of minutes, I'd walked into work and was being escorted out. There were no good-byes and no e-mail farewells to employees. They told me that they'd pack everything I'd accumulated over the last 12 years and send it to my house. The lock to my office had been changed overnight, my password was already wiped out of the company network, and I was gone.

That evening, I sat shell-shocked and sniffled over dinner with my daughters at the neighborhood cantina. "How could they?" I asked, swigging down a Corona. "Look at everything I did for them. Look at how many times we moved." I couldn't believe that this was how they repaid me.

"They're going to be sorry," said loyal, good-hearted Melissa. "When they ask you to come back, it will be too late because you're going to be in a better place."

"I never liked ADT anyway," said her irreverent, competitive younger sister, Jennifer. "But please, Dad, take my napkin. Your taco salad is going to be toast if you don't catch that snot ball." In other words, quit feeling sorry for yourself, Dad. They did you a favor.

My daughters could see the silver lining in the dark cloud which hung over me, but I couldn't—not yet, anyway. But down the road, I can see that my girls were right. The bad news truly was a blessing in disguise, causing me to steer off my present course and blaze a new trail, one that I wouldn't have explored had I not received the good news, bad news that morning.

You probably have gone and will go through tough times. As Robert Schuller once said, "Tough times never last, but tough people do!" It's not the bad news itself that creates havoc in your life, but rather, your reaction to it. Will you sit and sulk and feel sorry for yourself, like I did, or will you pick yourself up and figure out how to use it as a launching pad toward something bigger and better? This is one time when you've been thrown a curve ball, but now you're in a position to do something with it. How you respond will determine whether that bad news was really bad news, or if it was a gift—an opportunity to take your marathon to the next level.

It's your marathon—run it. Don't let the circumstances and events along the way run it for you.

Exercise:

What would you do if you were suddenly given an opportunity to do something different? Would you change careers entirely or start your own business? Have a backup plan ready, just in case you're involuntarily thrown off course and map out the steps you'll need to take to make it happen. Then, when somebody says, "And I've got bad news," your glass will be half full and you'll be ready. Instead of sulking over a Corona, you'll be celebrating the favor you were just given, even if you didn't know you wanted it.

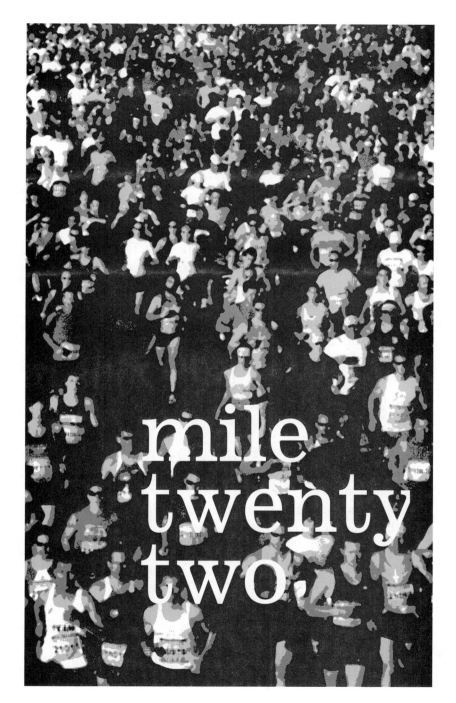

mile
twenty
two

Surround Yourself with Positive People

"Perpetual optimism is a force multiplier."

Colin Powell

Walk into a room of smiling people, and you'll smile, too. Sometimes, you won't even know why. On the contrary, if you walk into a room of subdued people, you'll mirror their behavior, too. You have a tendency to mimic the people around you—and that goes for their success, as well. Think about it; if you hang around with a bunch of negative people who are uninspired to do anything with their life, you're probably going to adopt their bad habits. However, if you associate with positive people who are excited, energized, and striving to make great things happen, you'll find that their attitude rubs off on you. Enthusiasm is contagious.

It's true that pessimists bring you down to their level, sharing their 'woe is me' attitude and their acceptance of it. That's the bad news. The good news is that optimists can also bring you up to their level, where the world is rosy and full of abundance and opportunities at every turn. Where would you rather be?

Motivational speaker Jim Rohn is famous for his observation: "You are the average of the five people you spend the most time with." It's surprising how much impact the people you surround yourself with have on your daily life and your success. They have more influence over your life and outcomes than any other factor or event.

Imagine yourself running along on your marathon, and you reach a point where the road gets a little bumpy. It's getting hot, and you're quickly feeling your energy wane. You're tired and achy and the finish line seems like an eternity away. You have two choices—push through it or quit.

If your fellow marathoners are all dropping like flies, saying it's too hard, they can't do it, you're likely to join them. On the other hand, if you're running with people who are determined to finish their marathon and claim victory, you'll be inclined to keep going, fueled by their determination and excitement, as well as their belief that they can cross that finish line.

The difference is a positive attitude. Optimism makes you see possibilities; pessimism limits your vision to improbabilities. If you can't see it and believe it, you can't achieve it.

When ADT let me go, I was in a unique position and found myself looking at a major career move. Suddenly, I had to surround myself with new people in a totally new line of work. One of those people made a world of difference in the outcome of my success.

Forrest was about 45; he had thick glasses, thinning hair, and an open, contagious smile. He'd been in outplacement for about four months before I arrived that morning. Admittedly, I was still off stride after losing my job in the corporate merger.

"Welcome to the executive orphanage," he happily greeted me, breaking in on my pity party. "You want me to show you around? The coffee wasn't great, so we decided to take turns bringing in beans from Starbucks, and some of us chipped in for snacks."

Forrest said, and truly believed, you could accomplish anything if you put yourself in a positive frame of mind. He saw win-win opportunities in every situation. When I was around him, it was hard to feel sorry for myself and be a poster child of doom and gloom. He was just what I needed at that stage in my life, and 15 years later, I am still thankful he came into my life.

In my former position, I had often been called upon to speak at sales conferences and industry association meetings. Forrest encouraged me to seek new opportunities from that experience. He became my new one-man audience, cheering me on and assuring me that I had special talent. He believed in me and gave me the confidence to embark on a new leg on my marathon. So much so, that one morning, he arrived with an ad he clipped from the Atlanta Journal Constitution inviting aspiring speakers to try out for public speaking seminars.

I don't know if I would have done it without him, but Forrest was so optimistic and positive that I couldn't help but feel his enthusiasm as well. He helped me put together a portfolio, laughing at the photograph we'd chosen of me crossing the finish line of the Atlanta marathon. "This half-naked shot will put you way ahead of the pack," he said.

When audition day arrived, Forrest came along for support. I might have turned around when I saw the line of people winding around the convention center if Forrest hadn't been at my side, reminding me that I could do this and that I did, indeed, have talent. By the end of the day, two people were selected from more than 300 to go on to become public speakers. I was one of them, but I couldn't have done it without the help, and the positive attitude, of my friend, Forrest.

Take a look at the people surrounding you. Are they positive or negative? Do they raise you up or bring you down? Do they discourage you from trying new things, or do they inspire you to accomplish them? You are the company you keep—seek the company of those who will impact your life in positive ways, and you'll make positive things happen on your journey.

Exercise:

Write down the names of the people you associate with most. Define their mind-set—are they positive or negative? Rededicate your time, choosing to spend more time with the positive people on your list and less with the negative. (If you don't have positive people on your list, it's time to run out and start meeting more people and making new friends!)

1.

2.

3.

4.

5.

6.

mile
twenty
three

Honor the Fallen

"We come, not to mourn our dead soldiers, but to praise them."

Francis A. Walker

We meet them every day—those who have served our country with honor and dignity. They are our brothers, sisters, relatives, friends, and neighbors. They are community leaders and fellow citizens. They are our heroes.

Risking their lives, these heroes work tirelessly, doing their duties without complaint and with little praise. They spend long stretches of time away from their loved ones, sacrificing their lives for the sake of improving and saving the lives of others less fortunate. Some are fresh out of high school and not even old enough to legally buy a beer—others have paid their dues and are at the end of their journey in a nursing home or Veteran's home. Still others have made the ultimate sacrifice and have joined the many who have fallen before them. They, too, are our heroes.

From public servants, like firefighters and police officers, to the brave men and women who serve our country in the Armed Forces, there are heroes amongst us. Some are living, and I encourage you to thank them for their service and the sacrifices they make every day to make your journey a safe and free one. Then, there are those who have lost their lives, either in the line of duty or after serving it. Their loss is great, and their memories are ingrained on monuments and in the hearts of those who knew and loved them.

There's always time in your marathon to honor these heroes. Regardless of what role they played, each and every one of them has made a difference in the lives of their fellow man. Without them, your marathon would not be possible.

Aaron made a difference. He also made the ultimate sacrifice.

Aaron was his single mother's only child. As a teenager, he dreamed of becoming a soldier, and he enlisted in the Army straight out of high school. After his second tour in Iraq, he returned home, full of nervous energy like always, fiercely loyal to his mother, and still intensely curious about people and his environment. "When he entered a room, everyone felt it," Aaron's mother said. "The energy picked up. People would become more animated."

Her voice on the phone line was soft and distant, but the undercurrent of prideful emotion was unmistakable. She had recently returned home from Colorado where she'd dispersed her son's ashes into the winds atop Pikes Peak.

"He would want me to be fully alive, fully engaged in life," she said. "Life was an adventure for Aaron. He was present in every moment, and that's how he'd expect me to continue on."

Since his return, there were moments when Aaron went inward and seemed to disappear. When asked if something was wrong, he would shrug off the inquiry and shake his head. Nine weeks after returning home, Aaron died of a self-inflicted gunshot from a handgun he purchased in Houston a month before. No one knew he had it; he hadn't told his mother, his friends, or his girlfriend with whom he'd argued moments before he took his life.

"He was an impulsive boy," said his mother. "Sometimes he'd act without thinking. I can just hear him saying to himself, 'Oh darn,' when the gun went off. That would be just like him." She regularly joins other parents at memorial ceremonies held to honor sons and daughters lost to the wars in Iraq and Afghanistan. Together, they share stories about their children: the soldier who died in the streets of Fallujah protecting his unit, the daughter with the Texas A&M degree who died in the explosion of a roadside bomb.

"Some people might say Aaron took the easy way out from his troubles," said his mother. "But I don't believe that, and neither do the other mothers who have lost their children. He is as much a hero as anyone who has served our country in the military."

I was in the Air Force, and I've witnessed the courage and bravery of those who have served our country. Their duty has been indelibly scratched into their lives forever. Like me, they considered it not only their obligation to serve, but also an honor. I encourage you to honor them. Honor your firemen and policemen. Honor our country's soldiers. Honor the fallen. Their service and sacrifice, no matter how large or how small, mattered.

All gave some,
Some gave all,
Always remember.

mile
twenty
four

Create Leaders

> "Leaders don't create followers,
> they create more leaders."

Tom Peters

In every marathon, there's a leader—the person who sets the pace and leads his fellow runners across the finish line. He inspires others to follow in his footsteps, so that they, too, can one day be just as fast and just as strong and someday lead their own marathon.

These leaders are everywhere in your life. They're teachers, athletes, managers, business owners, and public servants. They know that they have responsibilities to their home, their organization, and their community. One of those is to encourage and permit others to become leaders, as well.

Vince Lombardi once said, "Leaders aren't born, they are made." They got where they are by learning from the leaders who influenced their marathon. Those leaders were role models who propelled them to move forward, seek solutions, and develop their own leadership skills.

Think about it. The greatest leaders in your life probably didn't tell you what to do—they showed you how to do it so you could complete the task easier. They are the ones who live by the 'fish' principle: Give a man a fish, and he'll eat for a day. Teach a man to fish, and he'll eat for a lifetime. In essence, what they are doing is creating leaders, not followers.

When you create leaders instead of followers, it's a whole

new marathon. Everybody runs together at an even pace. They are all marathon fit and happy to put their best foot forward to benefit the cause. As the Marathon CEO, this concept is one I emphasize as I travel the country and share my message with audiences from coast to coast. When I do, it's not unusual for me to bring up Jack.

Jack's company had been hit hard by the economic downturn, and he decided to meet with his employees to get their perspectives on the state of the business.

Here's what he saw:

- Fear – people were still upset by last year's layoffs

- Fatigue – with a smaller workforce, everybody's work load was heavier than ever

- Stress – they were feeling the strain of last year's pay cut

Jack had built up some decent leadership skills on his marathon, but he was hitting a wall and he needed to dig deeper. "You're a good leader, Jack," I told my old Air Force buddy when he called for advice. "Now, you need to become great."

So, what's the difference between good and great leadership?

A good leader gets people to...well...follow the leader (remember Simon Says?). A great leader instills confidence in others so they can go forward on their own steam and become leaders in their own right. If you can help others create their own vision of success, you can transform fear, fatigue, and stress into commitment, purpose, and positive energy.

Jack needed to do more than get people to follow him

blindly—he needed to create leaders. Then, they would also take pride in their role and work side by side with him to ensure that they got the outcomes they wanted.

People take pride in running their own marathons, making conscious decisions that support their own YOU, Inc. They hold themselves responsible for their own personal fitness—mentally, emotionally, physically, and spiritually—and gladly set the pace as they propel their organization toward its goals.

There's more to being a leader than being the boss. So, whether you want to go an extra mile, dig deeper, or pull yourself or your company out of a slump, create leaders. They'll understand and appreciate their own value as leaders on the course. They'll want to help you and will take it upon themselves to make the company and themselves marathon fit.

Remember, good leaders create followers; great leaders create great leaders. Which would you rather have?

mile twenty five

Appreciate and Value Other Runners

"Appreciation is a wonderful thing.
It makes what is excellent in others
belong to us, as well."

Voltaire

Looking out for number one is important; after all, you are the only one charged with the responsibility for your happiness, health, and success. But there are times in your marathon when you'll be called upon to appreciate the contributions of other runners. Look at all the people you come in contact with every day and clearly see how their presence has benefitted you. They all have something unique to offer—a kind word, advice, lessons, and good deeds that make your marathon easier. Of all of these, it is perhaps not what other people do for you that is most remarkable, but the lessons they can teach you.

There will be times when others will give you advice, often unsolicited, which might be appreciated or resented. If you appreciate it, say so. If you don't, don't rush to judgment and dismiss their contribution. For I've found that, oftentimes, it is the things you don't know that you needed to learn that become most useful later in your marathon. Only then, do you have the hindsight to look back and say, "Now I get it. He was right." It may be days, months, or years later, but down the road, you'll find a time when the relevance of their contribution will become evident and valuable. As Voltaire said in the quote above, appreciation for others, even those who don't hold the same views or values that we do, is a way for us to own some of their excellence.

It was a late night in November of 1971 when I finally completed my program. I walked out of the computer science lab at the USAF Academy carrying the culmination of two weeks of work, over 200 punch cards. I was just a freshman, or a doolie as we were called, as I ran along a marble strip through the falling snow back to my dorm. As luck, or the lack of it, would have it, I lost my footing and began to fall backwards. As if in slow motion, I watched my books and my stack of punch cards fly into the air. I remember yelling something about horse manure as I went down and saw the rubber bands holding the punch cards together snap and break, throwing weeks of hard programming work to spin and fly away into the cold night air. I was beside myself, muttering in frustration at my clumsiness and the elements for letting such a stupid thing happen.

Then I heard an upperclassman's voice behind me, commanding me in no uncertain terms to "GET BACK IN MY BRACE." Great, now not only had I lost all of my hard work, but I'd also compounded my problem by losing my composure under stress. To make matters worse, my behavior was caught by a very strict, regulation-abiding, no-slack-cutting, I-don't-give-snowstorm-breaks kind of guy. Ouch.

I was sentenced (yes, sentenced) to goon squad for the weekend, so I got to march tours all weekend instead of going to Denver, where I really wanted to be. That was a devastating blow to a struggling doolie who only got two weekends a semester to leave campus, and now I'd just lost one of them. Needless to say, I didn't blame myself entirely—I gave some of the credit for my situation to the upperclassman who called me on it. I despised Cadet 2 Class C.B. "MUSHROOM" BURGER III (that is how I referred to him then), from Dennison, Texas, for the rest of my four years for not giving me a break on that occasion. Because of him, I was imposed the only restrictions I ever faced at USAFA. It didn't matter that he had taken the time to explain to me that as future pilots/leaders, we would have to be able to keep our cool in an emergency or crisis situation, and that I had totally lost mine that night.

It was 38 years later when I was able to appreciate the value and relevance of what he was trying to teach me. On the evening of January 15, 2009, I watched the evening news and heard a familiar command...BRACE...for impact...from a voice and a name that sounded eerily familiar. I looked up and, sure enough, there he was....the C2C from my past...Captain Chesley B. Sullenberger (aka Mushroomburger, to me) III from Dennison, Texas, who had just saved the lives of 155 people by safely landing a plane on water. The man who I had blamed for my restrictions was now the HERO of the Hudson. The calm, focused manner in which he carried out his actions that day demonstrated to me that he was a man of his words. He not only spoke them; he lived them. They had become a part of his excellence, and he had been trying to share that excellence with me back in 1971.

Do you have a Captain Sullenberger in your life—someone who tried to teach you something that you didn't think you needed to know? Someone who gave you unsolicited advice or who you didn't appreciate because you felt they were different, difficult, or even annoying at the time? No two runners are the same. That doesn't mean that we can't value and appreciate those who aren't like us and learn to accept the unique excellence that they share with us in our marathons.

You may not know it now, but 38 years later, you might just see the value in the words they speak and live by.

mile
twenty
six

Be Thankful

"Lauren was a gift."

Sharon Matte

In this marathon we call life, we often get too wrapped up in our day-to-day activities to take the time to appreciate the beauty, generosity, and people who have blessed us. If you're like me, you know how easy it is to get up and go to work, take care of your family and home, run errands, and before you know it, the day is done. Looking back, you didn't have an opportunity to appreciate any of it. You did your job without pausing to be thankful that you had one. You ate dinner with your family, but took the food and the company for granted. You conversed with a good friend and hung up the phone without letting them know how much you appreciate them in your life.

Life sometimes gets too busy and routine to remember to be grateful for the things and the people who are part of our marathon. Yet, we all have reasons to be thankful—for our health, the love of our spouse and children, a good friend, the generosity and kindness of a stranger, our job, and the place we call home.

Reasons to be thankful even come in unexpected forms. There are times in life when it's not easy to find something to be thankful for—especially when tragedy strikes. That's how I used to feel, until one very special lady changed my viewpoint forever, reminding me that those are often the times when we should be most thankful.

I'd been dating for a while when I finally met Sharon. Our first date consisted of lunch at a local restaurant, where we got to know more about each other.

As we talked over our salads, Sharon told me she had two daughters - Megan and Lauren. Megan, she said, was an eighth grader who loved to dance. In turn, I proudly displayed photos of my daughters, Melissa and Jennifer. Our conversation flowed easily, and it seemed like we were making a nice connection. I then asked about her other daughter, Lauren.

Sharon paused a moment and put down her fork. "Lauren," she said, "was a gift I received for almost 13 years. She was also a dancer as well as a runner. One morning in March of 1995, when I went to get her out of bed for track practice, she didn't wake up."

Her words caught me off guard and then some. Sharon had shared her daughter with me with so much grace and love that I was moved to tears. Excusing myself, I left the table, feeling an urgent need to do something I hadn't done in a long time—call my daughters and tell them how much I loved them - what a gift they were.

I realized that day that I had met a special woman— someone who chose to be thankful for one of her greatest gifts, rather than dwelling on the fact that she had been taken too soon. Through her, I learned how important it is to appreciate the people in my life and to be thankful for them every day.

Today, I am thankful to have Sharon as my wife, and I'm also thankful to be blessed with two beautiful daughters, as well as two beautiful stepdaughters: Megan and Lauren, the gift Sharon first shared with me 11 years ago.

What gifts have you received on your marathon? Take a moment and be thankful for them for some gifts are far too precious to take for granted.

the
last
two
tenths

Still Running...

"You're in your marathon for the
long run—your lifetime."

Mike Matte

At some point in your marathon, you begin to realize that there might be a few activities that have gone to the wayside in your life, perhaps never to reappear. It's a strange feeling, I guess what you might call a dawning sense of mortality when you face the reality that you might not always be able to do everything you once could.

A friend of mine was first awakened to this concept on a Monday morning at work when she told her boss how much she had enjoyed her weekend skiing in Vermont. The boss—whom she admired—a man who would three years later run a marathon—responded with wry humor. He said that, having reached the age of 40, he had come to realize there were certain things he would never experience in his lifetime, and skiing was one of them. She was incredulous in her reply, "You're kidding?!"

On January 13, 2008, I had no inkling that the Houston Half Marathon would be my last. Before the race began, I went through my regular ritual, meditating in the cold, dark port-a-potty. I visualized the moment I crossed the finish line, the exhilaration, the cheers, the shock of ice water thrown from the coolers, the sound of the race official calling my name and number over the microphone, and the proud smile on my wife's face.

I ignored the guy outside who was banging on the door. "When are you coming out of there, man? Your turn is over. We're all nervous. Come on, there's a line out here."

It was 41 degrees downtown, and 25,000 people had gathered to watch the race.

Moving along to the starting line, I reflected on how beautiful winter is in Houston. There wasn't a hint of humidity, and the sun was shining bright.

My number put me about 100 feet behind the starting line. The pistol went off, and the throng stirred in anticipation. "Come on, come on. Let's get going." We were ready. Finally, we started to move...

I completed the half marathon; everything I had visualized became reality. When it was over, I was ready to plan my next marathon. But something happened to make me realize that I wouldn't always be able to enjoy some activities—I guess you could call it one of life's unexpected events.

I took a misstep off a curb in Dallas and immediately felt a twinge in my hip. When the pain worsened, I saw an orthopedic surgeon, and it was at that point that my marathon took me head-on into the unexpected. I needed a partial hip replacement, fast. They said I might not ever run again. I had hit the wall—a massive one.

Eleven months after running the Houston Half Marathon, I lay on a gurney, looking up at my orthopedic surgeon. "Now, Mike, I have to ask you this question for liability purposes," he said. "Tell me which hip."

I pointed to my right and immediately felt the cold felt Magic Marker glide across my skin. The unmistakable sweet chemical odor of indelible ink pierced the air of the operating room.

Several hours later, I woke up with a hip made of Birmingham steel.

I was determined that I would run the Houston Half Marathon in 2010, but the pain was too much. By the time I settled for the 5K, it was too late – the roster was already full.

So on January 17, 2010, I set out on my own 5K, this time running away from the crowds, instead of with them. I ran along Buffalo Bayou, up the grassy slope to Waugh Drive and headed west toward Memorial Park. It was a beautiful winter day in Houston. There wasn't a hint of humidity, and the sun was shining bright. And I was still running.

It is my fondest hope that you are, too.

Mike Matte's Marathon

Known by many as the Marathon CEO, I've been running most of my life. For the past 25 years, I've worked with more than 40 companies and business units as CEO, President and General Manager, leading their financial and operations turnarounds by creating highly motivated employee teams. Along the way, I've realized that many of the same traits and skills necessary to run and finish a marathon apply to leadership and life. As a speaker, I call them the 26.2 Principles— you can think of them as 26.2 Marathon Mile Markers for Success in the Long Run—your lifetime.

My marathon has taken me across this great country, where I've had the honor and the privilege of serving in the Air Force. I've met many talented people as I've worked with different companies across the nation, and as a public speaker, I share the knowledge and experience I've gained to help others improve their performance on all levels.

Throughout my life, there have been many changes, but if there is one constant, it has been my love of running. Here are some of the personal mile markers in my marathon:

> *1967:* I began my track career as a high school freshman. A small-town 'coach's kid' from northern Illinois, I set the school record for the mile, running it in 4:45.6 minutes on an old cinder track.

> *1969:* I switched to the half mile, setting another school record of 1:59.0, which qualified me for State. An athlete, I was also quarterback of the high school's

football team, which won 44 games in a row between 1968 and 1972. I turned to running to relieve the pressure that came with being a 145-pound football player, an undersized kid in a small town. During my high school years, I also played point guard on the school's basketball team.

1971: Having received a Congressional appointment to the U.S. Air Force Academy, I ran out of my hometown on July 4, 1971, into an eight-year military career. While in the Air Force, I ran for food—literally. Members of the cross country/track team were allowed to eat at athletic team tables, a place where doolies could actually eat. The others sat at regular squadron tables and were required to sing five verses of "The Air Force Song." My track stint in the Air Force also gave me a reason to persevere when 48 percent of my class fell victim to the pressures and controversy surrounding the Viet Nam War and dropped out of the Academy.

1975 – 1980: My active years of duty were spent running B-52 flight-line weapons squadrons with up to 200 aircraft technicians. I was a weapons officer in Arkansas and Guam. Working six to seven 12-hour days per week, I temporarily stopped running and ultimately gained 35 pounds before my father's heart attack became my wake-up call and inspired me to lace up my running shoes again.

1980: I left the military and using the education and experience I gained in the Air Force, fast-tracked into a general manager position in Cincinnati. At 27 years old, I was the youngest person in a 30-person office and faced with the challenge of turning around a company that was losing revenue. Once again, I became a workaholic and stopped running. Denis Waitley's

Psychology of Winning program got me and the company back on track. I turned the company around and dusted off my running shoes, setting a goal of qualifying for the Boston Marathon.

1984: I met my goal! Running the Chicago Marathon in two hours and 48 minutes (my personal best) qualified me for the Boston Marathon.

1994: I continued to move from place to place, relocating 16 times to face the challenges of turning around a dozen more companies/profit centers.

1997: After 12 successful years, I lost my job when ADT let all five divisional presidents go on the same day.

1997 - 1998: A time of change, I spent a year in Atlanta in executive outplacement (i.e., executive orphanage for terminated lost souls). I auditioned for a public speaking position in 1997 and began speaking in public workshops across the country.

1998: Another move, this time to Texas, where I became President of a Fort Worth company. A good year, I met my second wife, Sharon, and turned around three more companies over the next 10 years.

Today, I call Houston my home. I am now a full-time speaker and a running grandfather. I put my running shoes back on in 1980 and haven't stopped running since—even when I needed a hip replacement and was told I might never run again. To date, I've run in over 400 road races and seven marathons.

In 2010, I was honored and privileged to be named as a Director of the USA Track and Field Foundation, where I hope to lend my military, athletic, and business experience to provide others with the same life skills, benefits, and opportunities that running has provided in my life's marathon.